CHILD~ as Volunteers

Preparing for Community Service

Illustrations by Pat Achilles

Susan J. Ellis
Anne Weisbord
Katherine H. Noyes

Acknowledgements

We would like to note that the original edition of Children as Volunteers published in 1983, credited Trina Tracy and Lawrence Wallace as contributors. They conducted many of the original interviews with children and helped to formulate the basic recommendations of the first edition. Their work is still important to this version.

We are indebted to Jeffrey Kahn for his expertise as an attorney in reviewing the chapter on legal issues to make sure we are up-to-date for the 1990s. And we thank Diane Landis of United Way of America, Cynthia Parsons of SerVermont, Irwin Siegelman of Weekly Reader Corporation, and Paula Beugen of the Minnesota Office on Volunteer Services for their most helpful input as reviewers of the manuscript.

And thanks to Cara Blank for her electronic publishing wizardry in 2003!

ISBN 0-94576-26-0, Third edition, 2003 — print
ISBN 0-94576-30-9, Third edition, 2003 — electronic

ISBN 0-940576-11-2, Revised Edition, 1991
Library of Congress Catalog Card Number 91-75388

ISBN 0-940576-05-8, Original Edition, 1983

PRINTED IN THE UNITED STATES OF AMERICA

Contents

1 Think Young 1
   Why a Revision? 2
   Who Are Our Readers? 3
   What Age Do We Mean? 3
   Vocabulary 4
   The "Mandating" Controversy 5
   What this Book Is Not...and Is 7

2 Kids' Eye View 9
   Interview Question 1: 9
   "What do you think of when you hear the word 'volunteer'?"
   Interview Question 2: 11
   "What does 'community service' mean to you?"
   Interview Question 3: 11
   "What have you done as a volunteer?"
   Interview Question 4: 13
   "How did this volunteering make you feel?"
   Interview Question 5: 16
   "What kinds of volunteering could kids do if given the chance? What would you like to do?"

3 Not a New Idea 19
   Historical Perspective 19
   Contemporary Perspective 21

4 Welcoming Children 27
   (Especially for agency leaders of volunteer programs, but worthwhile for leaders of children, too.)
   Benefits to the Agency 27
   Options for Involvement 28
   Preparing Your Organization 29
   Input from Children 30
   Designing Assignments for Children 32
   Writing Job Descriptions 33
   Preparing for Special Needs 35
   Recruitment 36
   Teacher/Group Leader Role 39
   Interviewing and Screening 40
   Scheduling 43
   Orientation and Training 43
   Supervision 45
   Recognition 46

5 Volunteering Children 49

(Especially for teachers and other leaders of children, but worthwhile for leaders of volunteer programs, too.)

Choosing What to Do 49
Everyone Benefits 49
Choice 50
Options for Service 50
Independent Projects 52
Linking with Existing Efforts 52
Point Person 54

6 Legalities and Liabilities 55

Federal Child Labor Laws 55
State or Licensing Regulations 56
Insurance 57
Liability Waivers 58
Parental Consent 59
Protecting Children 59
Exploring Your Own Situation 61
Don't Worry! 62

7 Families Together 63

(Especially for parents who want to explore volunteering as a family.)

Selecting Your Family Project 63
Offering Your Services 66

8 Building for the Future 67

Appendix A: Interview/Survey Sources 69

Appendix B: Resources & Bibliography 73

Information on Volunteer Management 73
Information on Youth as Volunteers 73
Bibliography 75

Think Young

Children are the citizens of tomorrow.
Children are the promise of the future.
Children don't know why something "can't" be done.
Children are an untapped resource.

Although such phrases that value children are repeated often enough to sound trite, in modern society we rarely give our youngest citizens the opportunity to contribute their ideas and talents. Even organizations that serve or advocate for children perceive them primarily as recipients of service. Child labor laws forbid most employment prior to age fourteen. The paid work that youngsters are allowed to do (delivering papers, mowing lawns, running errands) is encouraged more to teach responsibility than to utilize the potential of children.

Volunteering is the perfect way for children to be welcomed as productive, active members of a community. While many volunteer assignments do require credentials or prior experience, a great number offer the chance to try something brand new and value enthusiasm more than background. As volunteers, boys and girls can demonstrate their independent abilities and can handle work according to their actual skill level rather than be restricted by their age.

College students and teenagers are increasingly welcome in organizations. This book advocates the inclusion of even younger children. We recognize—and will discuss—the need for practical management techniques to integrate youngsters effectively into service delivery. Our position is that the effort is worth it. In addition to the obvious benefit of "more hands," fresh ideas and energy are just two of the other positive contributions children make to recipient organizations.

The benefits of including children as providers of service extend beyond today. In a very real sense, when we involve them as volunteers, we are preparing our youth to become active, responsible, caring citizens. We teach them to become producers as well as consumers.

In point of fact, children are already active in many volunteer efforts but, for the most part, their participation is largely invisible and therefore taken for granted. Children pitch in when adults need help with mass mailings, or at special events loading cars, setting up booths, carrying packages, and cleaning up—but where are these activities recorded and recognized officially?

The attitude seems to be that "kids help their parents" (not always voluntarily!) and the connection is rarely made to the way the children have helped the overall project.

Some organizations may feel that they have already made a formal effort to utilize the volunteer services of children. However, all too often, closer examination reveals that children are used for their bodies, not their minds. The proliferation of "a-thons"—bike-a-thons, walk-a-thons, rock-a-thons, etc.—do allow for youngsters to raise money and feel enthusiastic about a cause. But these activities rarely tap the ideas of those participating. The children provide energy and have fun, but their roles are extremely limited and there is no continuity or follow-up after the event. For those who want to do more meaningful volunteer work, we need to highlight and create options that will allow young people to feel proud that they are providing significant service.

This book describes actual examples of how children are already volunteering in many meaningful ways and presents concrete guidelines for those of you who want to venture into the area of youth volunteerism. As we all seek ways to maximize available resources, can we afford to overlook children? Here is an opportunity to pioneer a whole new view of our youngest generation.

Why a Revision?

In 1983 the first edition of *Children as Volunteers* was on the cutting edge in promoting the untapped resource of volunteers under the age of fourteen. Our intent was to stimulate creativity and encourage adults to see children as givers of service as well as recipients. Since then, this rather avant-garde concept has become a mainstream issue, largely because of a resurgence of interest in service-learning school curricula as a part of educational reform. A growing number of "intergenerational" programs are blending young people with older people to help solve social problems. The concept of parents and children volunteering together as a family has also attracted attention. Other forms of youth participation now include various types of youth service corps, court-ordered community service by youthful offenders, and projects involving "at risk" youngsters.

Another trend has been the development of national media campaigns and classroom materials to motivate new youth volunteer efforts and to support existing ones. A plethora of information about volunteer programs for high school and college age students has been emerging. Whole books and articles are devoted to creating meaningful experiences and credit-bearing internships for older adolescents. These are most often written for educators.

Children as Volunteers remains the only book focusing on volunteers *under the age of fourteen* and is unique in its perspective: that of the agency or community organization willing to be the placement site for children.

Much of the original content of the 1983 edition required no change and is included in this edition. However, to respond to more recent concerns a decade later, we did a thorough search of the updated literature and other resources. We interviewed a new sample of youngsters to verify our responses to the original interview questions about volunteering. We added a survey of agency leaders to determine their concerns (and interest!) in having children participate as volunteers. From the new data, we were able to revise and strengthen all of the techniques, suggestions, and guidelines in *Children as Volunteers*. We also have included discussion of vocabulary and the emerging debate about mandated community service.

It is clear that more and more youth will be participating in service projects—whether as individuals, in groups, or with their family members. The projects may be directly sponsored by a school or community organization or may be done independently. Regardless of how children become active, all parties involved need to be prepared in order to make the experience a successful one. We therefore felt that it was timely to revise this book to support those agency staff, youth leaders, and teachers who want to implement practical programs for children as volunteers.

Who Are Our Readers?

This guidebook is directed at two distinct audiences:

1. **Leaders of Volunteer Programs:**
   Anyone who has responsibility for developing and coordinating volunteer efforts in an agency, unit of government, or other setting. Also, officers of any all-volunteer organization or association seeking additional help and youth leadership with projects sponsored by their group.

2. **Teachers and Leaders of Children:**
   Any adult responsible for a group of children who wants to explore the possibility of enabling those children to become involved in their community, including: educators, club or troop leaders, or individual parents or guardians—and teenagers working with younger children.

Because we recognize that many of our readers are themselves parents who may be intrigued by the idea of volunteering with their own children, we have included a short chapter directed specifically at that point of view.

What Age Do We Mean?

For the purposes of this guidebook, we define "children" as fourteen years of age and younger. We chose age fourteen as the cut-off for two reasons. First, in most states, youngsters can apply for part-time working papers after their fourteenth birthday and so that seemed like a good point to stop considering them as "children."

Second, fourteen is approximately the age at which young people enter high school. High school is a very different world from elementary and middle school/junior high school; expectations are more "adult" from then on. Further, a great deal has already been written about high school volunteers and service-learning programs, while little has been written about volunteering by younger students.

In researching this book, we discovered that the word "youth" is used loosely by many authors but usually refers to teenagers and even college students, rather than including children of younger ages. Therefore, we have avoided the term "youth," since this book is really about children.

We are cognizant of the inappropriateness of discussing children as if they were an homogeneous group. Clearly there are vast differences between pre-schoolers, for example, and early adolescents (ages ten to fourteen). But it is also inaccurate to assume that all seven-year-olds are at the same developmental level. The subsequent sections will take such diversity into account and suggest ways to adapt techniques to younger and somewhat older children. But the ideal way to operate is to disregard age as much as possible and to look at each individual child in terms of his or her emotional, physical and intellectual readiness to try a particular task. This is exactly what a good volunteer program manager does for adults, and the principle applies to children as well.

Some adults are uncomfortable with the word "kids" as a reference to children. Most of the children with whom we spoke do not mind being called kids. In fact, those over the age of seven or eight vastly prefer it to being called "children." Titles incorporating the word "junior" (as in Junior Guide) got mixed reviews. There are no rules; each group of youngsters will have different preferences. If in doubt, ask children (kids) directly!

Vocabulary

Knowing that it is in vogue to refer to school-sponsored volunteering as "community service," we asked our 1991 interview participants what they thought of when they heard this term. One ten-year-old, in all seriousness, responded: "Community service is when you order a pizza and they deliver it to your house." This certainly highlights that words mean different things to different people!

As the involvement of young people expands, new vocabulary is applied by educators, writers, conference organizers, government officials, and agency representatives. Each has its own perspective and language, and makes value judgements about the others' terminology. This creates a new problem of selective listening and incompatibility, ultimately working against collaboration even on mutually-accepted youth volunteer programs.

We need to be able to talk with each other. Let's start by examining the most popular phrases currently used to describe some form of community involvement by young people.

Volunteering is the most commonly-used term for willingly contributing time and talent to a cause without seeking monetary profit. Regardless of how a person might originally sign up to become involved, from the perspective of the recipient agency or individual, the person is a volunteer because s/he is not on the payroll.

Although there is little argument with the above, there is resistance to applying the word "volunteer" to students. Educators (rightly) want to emphasize that students who receive academic credit for their participation need to have a thoughtful, educational experience. They see too much volunteer work that is "busy work" or nonskilled in nature and want to separate themselves from that image. There are also negative stereotypes about the word "volunteer," stemming from the historical perception that volunteers are simply pleasant helpers with little clout. If students are going to be enthused about service, it must be labeled to invoke pride.

Service-learning refers to curriculum-based service, and highlights that community involvement by students should be accompanied by an educational component. Ideally, service and learning are balanced.

Experiential education, or learning by experience, is another term often applied to student community work.

Service-learning, experiential education, internships, externships—these phrases almost always refer to student community work for academic credit. They also imply a structured feedback process to reflect upon the value and meaning of the field experience.

Community service is the term commonly used in federal, state, and local government initiatives emphasizing civic responsibility or citizen involvement. Many youth projects prefer the term community service, largely because it avoids the word "volunteer." However, this adds to the vocabulary confusion because "community service" is also the term used by the justice field for court-ordered or alternative sentencing programs.

Intergenerational programming is yet another label used to focus on those projects blending youngsters with older people. It is often purposely difficult to tell who is the giver and who is the recipient of service. For such programs, the goal is to attract participants of both ages, not to worry about who is the "volunteer."

Regardless of what adults want to call the activities, opportunities for young people to serve their communities are proliferating. But a common language must be found to be able to talk about projects, develop materials, approach funding sources, and create public policy. It will take time to overcome the barriers of politics and turf before there is universal agreement on the vocabulary used to describe youthful community involvement.

It also should be remembered that service by youngsters is not only organized through the schools. Many youth groups, religious congregations, community organizations, and individual families sponsor projects for which their boys and girls can volunteer. This type of participation is unrelated to formal academics and allows children to play a role in the community other than as "students."

For the purposes of this book, we will continue to use the term "volunteer" (both as a verb and a noun) because we think it is still the most appropriate word when considering the perspective of the recipient agency.

The "Mandating" Controversy

Having said that we will use the word volunteer, we next need to acknowledge that there is a growing movement aimed at mandating community service: requiring each student to do a certain number of hours of service in the community in order to complete course credit or to graduate. In some schools, the mandated service is incorporated into classroom curricula, while in others, students simply must document volunteer activities done on their own initiative. The majority of such programs are at the high school level but the trend is to extend the requirement down through kindergarten. The question on the minds of many is: if such service is mandated, is it voluntary?

Service-learning was long ago formalized as a requirement in the curriculum of many private schools, notably those run by religious groups such as the Society of Friends and the Jesuits. Some public school districts also have a long history of mandating community service, but in the late 1980s the concept became an issue in the nation's education reform movement. Advocates of required community service view

it as a vehicle to make education more relevant, motivate under-achievers, and lower dropout rates.

Educators and political leaders in states such as Minnesota, California, Vermont and Pennsylvania are paving the way to incorporate service-learning into their public schools—across all grades, kindergarten through twelfth grade. The emphasis is on designing curricula that teach the values of civic participation and service and then apply the classroom learning to real-life situations in the community. Curriculum materials to assist teachers are increasingly available from a wide variety of sources.

> From the United Nations Declaration of the Rights of the Child:
>
> Each child has...the right to learn to be a useful member of society and to develop individual abilities.

Since the time given to the community by students in such curricula is mandated, the label of "volunteer" does not even occur to some educators. The students themselves may feel coerced in having to complete the service requirement. Even some recipient agencies have difficulty viewing these students as "volunteers." They fear that mandating community service by students will be a deterrent that turns students off from future volunteer involvement.

In our opinion, mandating the performance of community service is not a problem if there are choices at every stage for the students to select the type of service they most want to do. For example, dictating that an entire class must paint a recreation room for a local agency is certainly not "voluntary." But giving students a long list of organizations seeking help, plus a variety of job assignments in those agencies, allows students to truly volunteer as to where they want to spend their time. Studies show that, when students choose their placement, a good percentage continue their service beyond the original requirement.

While some school districts resist mandating community service outright, the trend is definitely to "encourage" the concept of volunteering by students. Many schools offer options for students to participate in service projects, either as an alternative to course requirements or as an extracurricular activity.

From the perspective of the agency, students become part of the volunteer staff. They need all of the supports offered to any other volunteer (placement, training, supervision, and recognition) in order to have a satisfying experience. So, in practice, there are more similarities than differences between school-referred givers of service and any other volunteers.

Mandated community service may force teachers and students to turn to local organizations for placements, but there is no mandate for these agencies to accept students! Educators will need to develop relationships with agency leaders and project administrators. They must be prepared to communicate what students can do and to ask questions about supervision and training, transportation, insurance, etc. This becomes especially vital as younger and younger students are involved in service-learning.

Regardless of how you personally react to the concept of mandated community service, if it becomes a requirement in your local school district, you will be involved. We hope this book offers some useful guidelines for agency/school collaboration in order to take advantage of what volunteering is all about.

What this Book Is Not...and Is

This is not a comprehensive examination of how to manage a volunteer program, since resources already exist to cover such basics. This book does focus on how to adapt volunteer management principles in order to work effectively with children as volunteers.

This is not just a theoretical exercise. This book provides real-life examples shared by a wide variety of program managers and children themselves. The quotes highlighted throughout these pages testify to their experiences. Children were also critical to the writing of this book, both as survey/interview respondents and as advisors.

This is neither the first nor the last word on the subject of children as volunteers. But previous writing has tended to focus on specific, individual programs, while this book has a wider perspective. We offer new ideas. Our aim is to build your confidence so that you will join the growing number of adults who value the volunteer contributions of children.

Kids' Eye View

One basic premise repeated often in this book is: do not decide things *for* children; make decisions *with* them. We adhered to this philosophy in our original research and writing by arranging approximately twenty-five group interviews with more than 300 children. We talked with youngsters five to fourteen years of age, in and out of school settings, in urban and rural communities, and with a variety of racial, ethnic and economic characteristics.

For this revision, we interviewed an additional 54 children, again both urban and suburban, racially mixed, who were from nine to twelve years of age. We wanted to be sure that young attitudes and opinions had not changed significantly. Because of the popularization of the term "community service," we now asked the students what that term meant to them.

During the group discussions, we asked a range of questions about volunteering and community service. The children's ideas for specific service projects—ways to recruit other children, etc.—are presented later in this book, in the sections to which they relate. But many of the responses revealed how children perceive volunteering in general, based on their prior knowledge, stereotypes, and attitudes. Over and over again we found the youngsters to have a realistic understanding of who volunteers are and what they do. The new responses have been added to the original ones.

In response to all our questions, the definitions we heard were perhaps unsophisticated and the examples given were limited to personal experiences (as with adults!), but most responses were on target. Judge for yourself....

Interview Question 1:
"What do you think of when you hear the word 'volunteer'?"

Children are definitely familiar with the word "volunteer," though they may be limited in defining it. One connotation that was verbalized at almost every interview was: "when the teacher asks for help." In fact, one group of kindergarteners vied for the honor of receiving the title "classroom volunteer" because the word was big and adult-sounding. Other responses were clearly based on what children heard at home. Here are answers given by children in grades kindergarten to eighth grade—bet you can't tell who said what!

- *someone who helps somebody*
- *do something for the fun of it*
- *the fire department*
- *volunteer to fight*

- to join something
- join the Army/Navy
- doing it because you want to help the needy/poor
- give money
- take another person's place
- do a good deed
- to go without being forced
- a nurse
- a helper
- a banker
- telethons
- day care center
- police
- welfare
- helping old people
- food stamps
- adopt a child without parents
- a teacher
- a preacher
- to give food
- everybody
- donation collectors coming to your house
- wash dishes
- Candy Stripers
- working for nothing
- sacrifice
- charity
- help the handicapped
- thanks is the only pay
- older students tutor younger ones
- help God and myself
- lunch mothers
- a dance teacher
- teachers give volunteers part of their salaries
- see something that's needed in the system
- help out, especially when others are sick
- support others
- don't have to make money
- ambulance
- fool
- raise your hand or put a paper in the suggestion box
- willing to give up time for nothing for another person
- donator
- doing something for free
- help to sell things
- your own decision to do something to help people
- join football team to replace someone who's injured
- someone who helps cook
- teacher asks for help
- drive vans
- Indians helped Pilgrims
- free because you do it for love and not money
- join a club
- someone who cares
- someone who has something to do
- cheerleading
- something someone does in spare time
- singing club
- baseball
- school plays
- substitute teachers
- a worker
- sharing
- someone who saves a life
- problem solving
- babysitting
- donation of blood
- magic show audience
- help community
- working in school shop
- voting
- when you want to be a part of something
- someone who is not lazy

Unscientific though it is, this list seems to indicate that children see most health and safety professions as helpers and servers, and therefore volunteer-like. People who "substitute" are seen in the same way. There is some confusion about who receives a salary and who does not, which, of course, varies from community to community.

Interview Question 2:
"What does 'community service' mean to you?"

- *when people are asked to do something and they are helping people*
- *when somebody protects the neighborhood*
- *jobs in the community*
- *when you order pizza and they deliver it to your house*
- *like the Boy Scouts—when we help clean up*
- *help out old people who can't do stuff*
- *something they make reckless drivers do*
- *working at your local church*
- *it's what they make prisoners do*
- *helping handicapped people in the community, not people in a special school, but neighbors or individual persons*
- *community service is the whole community helping out*
- *when I first think about it, I think about people volunteering to help the community they live in and then when I think about it again, I think of when people have done something bad and are under age to go to jail, the police make them do community service*
- *community service is a type of volunteering*
- *help the community clean up the block*
- *same as volunteering*

It would seem that our respondents for the most part think of community service as a synonym to volunteering. There is some sense that community service involves or is offered to the entire community, as opposed to one-on-one. Additionally, some of the students were aware of the use of the term as applied by the courts in alternative sentencing.

Interview Question 3:
"What have you done as a volunteer?"

While some of the volunteer activities listed are quite creative, clearly most fall into the categories of home chores, errands, school activities, and fundraising. This tells us more about what youngsters were asked to do, than about what they might be willing to do (see Question 5). Some of the examples listed below are perhaps not "volunteering" as adults might define it, but certainly come under the umbrella of "helping"—an important part of the definition of the word volunteer as children see it.

- *day camp programs*
- *helped eat cupcake*
- *washed car*
- *took lost girl home*
- *helped give out announcements*
- *helped put little brother to bed*
- *mowed lawn for neighbor*
- *cleaned my room*

- joined football team
- help mom around the house
- substituted for cheerleader
- babysat
- washed sister's clothes
- walked for March of Dimes
- helped girlfriend study
- worked in the English Office
- collected for UNICEF
- block clean-up
- cleaned animal cages at museum
- painted sidewalks for Bicentennial
- dancing class at Y
- took part in a play
- made pizza for sports club banquet
- helped new bus driver with directions
- helped clean art room desks
- Girl Scout troop visited nursing home
- walked dog
- fed sister's horse
- washed the blackboards in school
- "Walk for Mankind"
- Pancake Day
- helped mother (choir director) with Christmas caroling
- called out numbers for bingo games at nursing home
- helped mom when she didn't feel good
- MS skate-a-thon
- Jerry Lewis thing
- sold magazines for school
- donated books to book sale
- raised my hand in class
- helped with fair booth
- cleaned cemetery
- went to the store for neighbor/old person
- helped push people in wheelchairs
- 6th grade ecology project
- helped newspaper boy
- made a card for a sick teacher in the hospital
- helped teacher pass out papers
- raked leaves
- helped sister with readingv

- had nothing to do, so picked up my clothes
- carnival face painting
- swim-a-thon
- helped in chapel
- shoveled snow
- safety patrol
- Candy Striper
- brought record to a friend
- took notes to office
- ball-boy for baseball team
- cheerleader opened doors for others
- watered plants
- washed windows
- behaved
- made party for teachers
- collected money for Christmas
- put tire on car
- replaced someone in a play
- put friend's dog back in cage
- collected clothes for drive
- sold hoagies (hero sandwiches) for soccer team
- played guitar for others
- friends sang for first graders
- brought in wooden horses for show-and-tell
- altar boy
- took care of pets while owners were away
- took first grader to bus stop
- set up chairs
- drew pictures to hang on wall
- served meals to old people in retirement home
- cleaned up at fire station
- helped with kindergarten kids
- helped build a house
- helped make soup for the homeless
- put grocery bags in people's cars at store
- read Scriptures at church
- helped at Teen Center at school
- shopped for someone who could not get out
- showed new person around school
- helped with props for play

- *volunteered to be on swim team*
- *did yard work for older neighbors*
- *picked up litter*
- *judges' aide at gymnastics meet*
- *helped with retarded children at camp*

- *got over my shyness*
- *felt grown up*
- *liked the thank you*
- *bad; my sister didn't want to learn*
- *worthwhile*
- *proof of being Christian*
- *learned a lot*

Interview Question 4:
"How did this volunteering make you feel?"

- *good about helping*
- *happy*
- *good, because I did something for someone and they didn't ask*
- *like I'm doing the right thing*
- *know I'm doing something for someone else*
- *satisfied*
- *helpful*
- *productive*
- *caring for someone*
- *proud*
- *friendly*
- *using my talent*
- *enjoyed it*
- *proud of myself and school*
- *special*
- *kind*
- *people know you love them*
- *makes God proud*
- *liked doing it*
- *"better to give than to receive"*
- *needed*
- *showing love*
- *like a man*
- *someone has confidence in me*
- *bad; didn't know how to do it*

- *hard; sometimes people don't want to admit they need help*
- *glad*
- *kept me busy*
- *it was interesting*
- *easy to do*
- *nice to be with friends*
- *proud to be doing something someone else can't do*
- *learned about different people*
- *better*
- *generous*
- *like I could accomplish things*
- *that I was capable of doing a job*
- *fun! I worked, had the radio on and was dancing around and cleaning*
- *good, but sometimes I felt used; I volunteered to clean up but then they kept giving me more work*
- *good, happy for the team*

There are no surprises in this list of how volunteering made children feel, but consider how the responses echo the feelings of adults. For children, a real benefit of volunteering is to be seen as a resource for giving to others, rather than only as recipients of adult help. It seems "adult-like" to volunteer and that is very appealing.

Many colleagues knew about our work on this book and several of them shared their own personal experiences with us. Marcia Penn, former Director of the Virginia State Office of Volunteerism, told us about a speech given by her daughter at the age of thirteen about being a volunteer. Tracy Penn wrote the speech completely on her own and delivered it to an audience of adults in Richmond, Virginia. Here is a copy of the original "document." There is no doubt about how Tracy felt about volunteering.

Hello, my name is Tracy and I am 13 years old. I have been a volunteer almost all of my life. When I was 2, I volunteered for the first time. My mother was working at a school for the retarted, and I helped them with there crawling exercises. I like to work with children, and volunteering helps me do this. For instance, two years ago at the Va. State fair, I vollunteered to work at the booth for the ~~Dept~~ Commision On Children + Youth. We put on a puppet show. I found this rewarding because I, made some little kids happy, taught people about The Commission on Children and Youth.

In school sometimes we vollunteer to help other students who are behind in their work,

I made a list of the things I think are PROS and CONS of Vollunteering . . .

PROS of Vollunteerism

1) It offers you new experiences, like speeking here today, that you might not otherwise get.

2) It provides the oppurtunity to meet new + interesting people

3) It makes me feel happy to help someone so they can succeed.

Cons of Vollunteerism

1) Sometimes it is boring like when I'm stuffing envelopes.

2) Sometimes you miss out on doing something fun because you promised to Vollunteer.

3) Sometimes it is tiring, for instance one year I walked on the crop walk. But it really was a good thing because I had fun and I was able to help people.

4) Sometimes Vollunteering is frustrating like on Holloween when you collect for Unicef. And people won't give and they are angry at you for asking.

I really enjoy volunteering, because it is rewording, as well as a learning experience

Thank you

Interview Question 5:
"What kinds of volunteering could kids do if given the chance? What would you like to do?"

When we asked these questions, we spoke about meeting community needs beyond school and family. It was sometimes hard to get the discussion moving but, once started, the ideas flowed freely. Some children voiced skepticism about the feasibility of these ideas ever becoming real opportunities because, as one ten-year-old said: "adults don't trust kids...adults think they need professionals and don't listen to us." Most of the children felt that they and their peers could accomplish many projects, if given some training and the right tools. They readily acknowledged their need for more information and instructions, and never implied that children could tackle major problems alone. They resent, however, being excluded from participation on the grounds of lack of experience or skill—their attitude is "teach us so we can help."

The sincere desire of youngsters to be part of solving problems (big and small) is evidenced by the following list—as is their awareness of exactly what problems exist.

- *help orphanages*
- *clean up neighborhoods*
- *organize kids into groups to ride subways safely*
- *help with Scout awards*
- *give people attention*
- *act parts in school plays*
- *paint houses*
- *get people not to litter*
- *go shopping for neighbors*
- *decorate trees for Christmas*
- *solve crimes*
- *help handicapped*
- *help someone live a better life*
- *help solve problems*
- *help children with birth defects*
- *fight disease*
- *collect cans*
- *do artwork*
- *do math tutoring*
- *try to stop fights*
- *help people who are hurt*
- *be a nun*
- *visit people*
- *help someone who lost something*
- *help with babies*
- *sing at church*
- *take flowers to the hospital*
- *learn first aid*
- *help at home*
- *help organize a party*
- *keep down noise on buses by telling loud passengers to be quiet*
- *share smiles and be friends with strangers*
- *make signs and banners for church*

- *take homework to sick friends*
- *play games with others*
- *clean off graffiti*
- *share ideas*
- *bring in stuff for class experiments*
- *stop violence*
- *prevent crime*
- *stop the shooting of animals*
- *prevent fires*
- *pick things off the floor when you drop them*
- *save lives/be a police girl*
- *make clothes for the handicapped and the elderly*
- *wheel around people in wheelchairs*
- *give money to the poor*
- *help new students at school*
- *be a Big Sister*
- *do summer tutoring*
- *help with summer day care*
- *work with younger children*
- *volunteer job where we could learn something*
- *prevent child abuse*
- *give free lunches*
- *bring black people and white people closer together*
- *clean up ponds and streams*
- *hold a skateboard marathon*
- *build a motorcycle track*
- *operate a place for young kids to hang out*
- *make toys and things*
- *donate stuff*
- *fill potholes*
- *plow the city after a snow storm*
- *help kids stay off drugs*
- *stop people from smoking*
- *work around the hospital*
- *help old people cook and clean*
- *help elderly on the street, into their cars, up the steps*
- *wash cars*
- *help in a store*
- *read to little kids*
- *help the teacher teach*
- *shovel driveways*
- *do yard work*

There are not a lot of new ideas on this list. Even young children have enough social conditioning to list common examples of helping; they have had little encouragement to think innovatively. Part of the problem in our interviews was "going in cold." Adults would also have had difficulty in generating creative ideas for potential volunteering, if the question were asked out of context.

When we had the time to structure a serious brainstorming session with boys and girls, we were able to stimulate them to go beyond the obvious. As they began to catch the spirit of thinking hard about community problems, they grew more confident in suggesting ways in which children could participate in solutions. This confirmed our belief that children want to volunteer their minds (ideas) and not just their bodies (doing chores). Some of the more unusual items in the preceding list came from such in-depth brainstorming.

Not a New Idea

Yes, Virginia, there are children already active as volunteers. In every community today there are wonderful examples of the ways young volunteers contribute their services. Before we share contemporary stories, let's look at how children participated in the past.

Historical Perspective

American history supports the idea of children as volunteers, though rarely was that label applied in the past to the roles they played. The priorities of colonial Americans were simple: first, survival; and second, the gradual improvement of living conditions. Both priorities required collaboration and hard work on the part of everyone. As the frontier moved westward, settlers continued to find strength in cooperative effort. Communities relied on themselves because there was no other help around—and all members pitched in to accomplish necessary work. Children were no exception, since pioneer adults could hardly afford to overlook the resource of extra helping hands. Children were visible in activities ranging from communal land clearing to helping in emergencies to cooperative wolf hunts. [1]Such participation by children was more than doing chores; it required a voluntary commitment to the good of the neighborhood. It also combined necessary work with learning and a degree of fun.

As time passed, children were recruited for specific causes and movements, as a logical extension of their continued involvement in community life. Here are some chronological examples of activities clearly identifiable as "volunteer":

~ The abolition movement deliberately enlisted the services of boys and girls in the 1830s by forming Juvenile Anti-Slavery Societies which circulated "Petitions for Minors." Such petitions against slavery were signed by hundreds of youngsters and sent to Congress.

~ The temperance crusade organized hundreds of children's clubs, such as the 1842 Sons of Temperance. This was an effort to give children some influence over a problem that often victimized them.

~ During the Civil War, children on both sides aided in countless collection and sewing projects in support of their armies. They made bandages and bedding, and even produced ammunition. On Independence Day, many Northern children pledged their firecracker money so that vegetables could be bought for the soldiers. Documents of the time record that Southern boys and girls even took part in the nursing of the wounded, since army medical facilities were established in local homes.

~ In the second half of the nineteenth century, rural children were formed into "agriculture clubs," paralleling adult farmer alliances. These clubs taught new "scientific farming" techniques, but also provided the youngsters the opportunity to do community service projects.

~ In the late 1890s, a movement developed to counteract the unhealthy conditions created by industrialization in the cities. The efforts centered around "Children's Leagues" in which boys and girls were taught that physical and moral cleanliness went hand-in-hand. Members were expected to go home and participate in activities such as "cleaning days," and even to teach their elders how to use a broom. By 1901 almost 100 such leagues were active.

~ As part of the fight against tuberculosis, public schools across the country became involved in the "Modern Health Crusader" program, an attempt—amazingly successful—to instill good hygiene and health habits. Students earned promotions within an intricate scheme of feudal pageantry (from Page through Knight to a seat at the Round Table) by obeying long lists of hygiene rules. These included taking ten deep breaths a day, bathing twice a week, and avoiding pickles! By 1920, at least 7,000,000 children were "in fealty to hygiene."

~ In the 1920s, the National Safety Council (its members being volunteers) coordinated a major safety awareness effort in the schools. Student "safety committees" were formed everywhere to study safety hazards and assist in preventing accidents. The children themselves often solved specific safety problems with their own ideas.

~ The rise in juvenile crime during the 1930s and 1940s led courts to involve young people themselves in combating delinquency. Among techniques in vogue were juvenile juries and even units of boy sheriffs.

~ Both World Wars evoked tremendous outpourings of civilian volunteer efforts by people of all ages. Children played a vital role in scrap drives, bond sales, and assistance to soldiers' families. Boys and girls planted World War II "Victory Gardens" (or "An Acre for a Soldier" in rural areas) for food conservation and collected everything from tin foil to toothpaste tubes to make up for metal shortages. When President Roosevelt put out a special call for donations of critically-needed rubber, Boy Scouts gathered at service stations to plead with motorists to surrender their car floor mats.

~ The late 1940s and 1950s saw the rise of programs for conservation and beautification. This movement included projects for children and youth. Youngsters participated in roadside improvement contests and anti-litter drives.

Contemporary Perspective

Today many adults are rediscovering the rewards of encouraging children to be social contributors. The following is a list of *actual* projects in which children under age fourteen have volunteered. The examples come from all over the country and demonstrate the immense range of possibilities. Note how the following structural elements are combined in the various projects described, creating a diversity of program models:

~ Children volunteering as individuals or in groups.

~ Ongoing projects or one-time activities.

~ Formal programs within an established agency or informal projects created independently.

~ Help given to institutions or given to individual people (indirect or direct services).

~ Volunteering that is intergenerational (child with adult), peer-to-peer (children of the same age), or "mixed" children (children of one age serving children of another age).

The examples could have been clustered into categories, but we have chosen to present them randomly in a single list, mixing all types of settings and fields. The advantage to reading the entire list is its cumulative impact. Your creativity in meeting the needs of your situation may be stimulated by seeing the roles given to children in other settings. Our goal is simply to point out what others have done so that you can adapt the concept to your own services and populations.

A ten-year-old girl who had to deal with her own serious illness wrote and illustrated a pamphlet that was used to help other young children deal with their hospital stays.

A team of sixth graders made greeting cards for Meals on Wheels and corresponded with nursing home residents.

A twelve-year-old created a volunteer organization to help the homeless. His singular act of help mushroomed into a successful fundraising campaign including a shelter for the homeless.

\Kindergarteners and first graders constructed blue bird houses to try to boost the area's dwindling eastern bluebird population.

Fourth graders recycled aluminum cans and used the money to feed the hungry.

———————————

Eight-year-olds and senior citizens worked together to grow vegetables in a community gardening project.

———————————

Families served as park monitors to offer information to visitors, keep campsites clean, and maintain rules in state parks.

———————————

School children were recruited for a "Kid's Way" component of a United Way. They surveyed their peers about perceived community problems, then decided how to fundraise from youth and which services to fund.

———————————

A group of preteens wrote and performed drug and alcohol prevention programs and led an open discussion afterwards.

———————————

A group of children went door-to-door on Halloween collecting canned food; they later sorted the donations and prepared Thanksgiving baskets for the needy.

———————————

Eleven-year-old students were matched with residents of a nursing home; the boys and girls visited their assigned "grandparents" for an hour twice a month during school hours, and dropped in on their own to visit on weekends or after school. Once a year, the children brought their senior partners to school for Grandparents' Day.

———————————

A group of children repaired used toys to be distributed to the needy at Christmas time.

———————————

In cooperation with local police, a group of Boy Scouts patrolled the parking lots of shopping malls during the summer in order to watch for illegal activities.

———————————

Groups of youngsters assisted with state and local park maintenance by painting and cleaning park buildings, clearing underbrush, maintaining trails, and constructing exhibits from natural materials.

———————————

Early adolescents with learning disabilities and behavioral problems tutored younger students. For example, fifth graders with reading problems tutored second graders who were just beginning to read.

———————————

Individual classes adopted specific military units during Operation Desert Storm and corresponded with the service men and women, sent small gifts, and participated in welcome home parades.

Fifth graders researched local history, published a guide to their county, and restored a century-old school bell.

Eighth graders wrote and compiled a math textbook based on "real life" math problems; the students researched careers that interested them, interviewed adults in those careers, and worked out typical math questions that might be encountered in the various types of work surveyed.

> In 1982 when floods almost devastated Fort Wayne, Indiana, the sandbagging efforts of an estimated 30,000 students (some as young as age 8) caused the mayor to go on national television to say: "The kids saved Fort Wayne."

A fourth grade class improved their community by: studying the causes of pollution; locating areas in the community that endangered the health of residents; organizing a clean-up campaign; and educating others about town sanitation.

Elementary students helped out at their school by answering phones, assisting in the office during lunch hour, and processing books in the school library.

Five-year-olds teamed with their mothers to assist with a Spring orientation program for incoming kindergarten pupils and their parents. The teams of guides welcomed newcomers at the door and assisted with name tags. Then the adult guides escorted the parents to a meeting with the teacher while their younger counterparts took the new children to the library for a story and showed them the classroom they would occupy in the Fall.

Elementary and junior high students assisted the mainstreaming process and fostered a better understanding of their disabled peers by creating: a peer tutoring program; a class notes sharing system; a sign language club; and a joint swimming program involving both disabled and non-disabled youngsters.

Fifth and sixth graders staged an Easter Egg Hunt for nursing home residents and disabled pre-schoolers; half the class colored the eggs with the residents and hid the eggs outdoors; the other half helped the pre-schoolers and residents find the eggs. (Talk about multi-level volunteering!)

Figure 1: *Drawing by Matthew G. Noyes, then age 5, depicting an actual example of volunteering he had done.* The picture shows Matt and friends (ages 5 to 12) folding, stapling, and labelling a mass mailing for their neighborhood association (at Mom's request). Note stacks of flyers, "speed" of letter being tossed across table, and ponytail on friend "L"! Almost 1,000 pieces of mail were handled. . .and a good time was had by all!

Middle school students conducted a walk-a-thon to raise money for their local volunteer fire department. Other creative fundraising events handled by children included tricycle rodeos, haunted houses, and math-a-thons.

Sixth graders conducted a blood pressure screening clinic for teachers, custodians, and parents; they studied "heart health" and blood pressure problems, learned how to use the medical equipment, planned and implemented the clinic, and referred adults having blood pressure problems to a doctor.

A seven-, an eight-, and a nine-year-old collated and assembled 125 registration packets for a statewide conference on volunteerism.

Children aged nine and up served as reporters and writers for school publications, local newspapers, and national columns.

A Cub Scout troop arranged to conduct its monthly meetings at a senior citizen housing complex; the boys planned activities that would encourage resident participation, such as flag folding, seed planting, and crafts projects.

Fifth graders formed their own "corporation" to raise funds by selling items to family members and friends; they then donated the profits to a civic project selected by the class.

Three-to-five year olds teamed up with their mothers to visit nursing home residents who were severely depressed. The teams built relationships with the residents, took them for walks, and encouraged participation in activities.

A class of sixth graders became safety advocates after using a reading workbook that included a picture of a child experimenting with a candle. The class wrote letters of complaint to the publisher stating that small children should not be encouraged to play with candles. The publisher agreed to drop the material from future editions of the book.

Youngsters of all ages worked with artists in projects such as painting murals on public buildings.

Twelve-, thirteen-, and fourteen-year-olds from a tough inner-city school worked with civic and business leaders to identify community problems and examine possible solutions. They organized a neighborhood health fair, lobbied for the removal of abandoned buildings, and created a community garden.

Fifth and sixth graders ("teacher-ettes") helped with younger classes by correcting papers, making visual aids, assisting with coats and hats, and monitoring classrooms at lunch time.

Seventh grade students researched, wrote and produced a 45-minute documentary film about the role minority groups played in their town's history. The children conducted interviews, wrote the script, and operated all the filming equipment. The film was distributed to local schools, cable networks, and libraries.

> "I like volunteering because it lets me do more things. I can take charge of myself and make decisions and I can help people. I feel good doing something for someone else."
>
> — Stuart Gilfillen, age 9, South Hamilton, MA

A group of youngsters, ages ten to fourteen, wrote and taped a weekly news show for cable television, "translating the news so kids can understand it."

Emotionally disturbed youngsters, ages six to fifteen, led group tours of a farm center; they also helped care for the animals and assisted with a Saturday program for mentally and physically handicapped youth.

Fifth and sixth graders taught an introductory computer course for their parents and other adults as part of their school district's evening Community Education Series.

Students in sixth, seventh and eighth grade bilingual classes taught their native language to English-speaking elementary schoolchildren. They developed their own teaching materials.

What's happening in your community?

---

[1]The historical material in this section is based on *By the People: A History of Americans as Volunteers, Revised Edition*, by Susan J. Ellis and Katherine Noyes Campbell, Philadelphia: Energize, Inc., 2003.

Welcoming Children

(Especially for agency leaders of volunteer programs, but worthwhile for leaders of children, too.)

Have the preceding sections sparked your interest? Are you already working with high school and college volunteers and thinking about adding even younger ones? Once you seriously consider the possibility of involving children as volunteers, questions about exactly *how* to do it probably come to mind. All too often the many unknowns of working with this special group of potential volunteers stop program leaders in their tracks, and the idea never gets tried. However, as with all new program challenges, the steps of involving children become manageable when examined one at a time. There is no inherent reason why any setting cannot utilize children as volunteers in some capacity. Where there's a will, there's a way, and obstacles and objections are matters of perspective.

We stipulate that *this book assumes you already understand the principles of good volunteer management*. Implementing a children's component of a volunteer program follows the same process, in the same sequence, as does developing one for adults. There are different emphases, considerations, and techniques when the focus is on children, but the basics remain the same. These basics have been dealt with at length in many books and articles. If you are new to volunteer administration, we strongly encourage you to refer to such resources to expand your abilities as a volunteer manager in general. You may also want to do some reading in the youth development field. Then you will be best able to utilize this book.

Knowing that more youth volunteer projects exist now than when we wrote the original edition of this book, we decided to survey agency representatives for a "reality check." We were particularly interested in attitudes and concerns that hindered the initiation of volunteer assignments for children

This chapter takes each major volunteer program management task and describes how it would have to be modified to involve children effectively: issues to consider, areas for caution, and points requiring special attention.

Benefits to the Agency

It is really helpful to articulate for yourself and others the benefits of having young volunteers on your staff. Some are:

~ A fresh approach to problems

~ Energy and enthusiasm

~ Willingness to do detailed, repetitive or messy tasks

~ Nonbiased interaction with people

~ Visibility and good public relations for your agency

~ More helping hands

Now list specific advantages for your own agency. Answer the following questions:

- *Why does your organization want to involve children as volunteers?*

- *What are the benefits to your employees and to your clients or consumers?*

- *What are the risks?*

- *If your organization serves children, would it be judicious to have children also participate as volunteers?*

- *Would it assist you in your efforts to recruit adult volunteers to establish intergenerational volunteer teams?*

- *Are you committed to trying the idea because the potential for good results outweighs the initial difficulties you may encounter?*

Options for Involvement

Consider the options for ways to involve children as volunteers and the implications of each for your program.

Individual Children

Children can be recruited one by one for special talents and to match particular needs. This allows for more flexibility in scheduling and the children can be supervised one at a time.

Groups of Children

Recruitment, assignment and some supervisory responsibilities can usually be shared with a group's teacher, adult, or teen leader. The children may be scheduled all at once, allowing for concentrated supervision at planned intervals. Training time is reduced and larger projects can be tackled. Members of a group motivate each other.

Family Teams

Parents and children can be recruited to volunteer together for the same job, or variations on this theme. Perhaps you might recruit one parent and a child, whole families, teams of older and younger siblings, or even grandparents and their grandchildren. This option is the easiest to manage because of the additional supervision and guidance provided by the related adult. However, because of the parental relationship, you will need to ensure opportunities for the child to contribute independently as well.

Non-related Intergenerational Teams

Two different age groups of volunteers (can include matching teenagers with children or senior citizens with children) can be paired to do a job together. This model maximizes supervision of the child while clearly allowing each volunteer to contribute equally. Note still another variation: you can recruit a number of parents and their children, schedule them at the same time, and then create "teams" by mixing and matching non-related adults and children.

Preparing Your Organization

We do not want to be Pollyannas! Although we know the benefits of working with children as volunteers, we recognize that there are always concerns among administrators and staff members to whom this may be a new concept. It is best to address these worries, try to find solutions wherever possible and weigh the pros and cons of the seemingly unsolvable ones. But at least clear the air. Make it comfortable for doubters to state their feelings. Let them know that others have had similar anxieties in establishing the groundwork for children volunteering in their agencies.

Be alert to expressed and unexpressed reservations and attempt to deal with these as early as possible. Stereotypes and fears about children in general may be just as problematic as resistance to volunteers of any age. With administrators and staff, you might compile a list of "possible problems when we involve children" and then examine each problem more closely. Distinguish between initial, and therefore temporary, difficulties and possible ongoing concerns. Ask the staff to propose ways of handling each problem and assure them that you seriously listen to what they say. It is amazing how resistance fades just by giving people the chance to air their fears and by demonstrating that you understand and intend to deal with possible problem areas.

In our 1991 survey of directors of volunteers, we asked those who were not recruiting under-14 year olds, why they weren't. Their responses included the following:

This is an inappropriate setting for children.

We cannot expose our confidential records and information.

We don't have transportation for youth volunteers.

The nature of this work is very delicate.

Kids need more supervision than adults.

We just don't have the manpower.

It takes too much time and effort to recruit kids.

These are common concerns that often block forward thinking. Your goal is to separate facts from fears. For example, the issue of transportation may very well be a legitimate problem and you need to apply managerial problem-solving techniques to it (see page 31). But to address fears, you face the more difficult challenge of changing attitudes— helping people to broaden their perspectives. For example:

~ In a setting that may seem "inappropriate" because children are not part of normal service provision, point out supportive tasks that might be done. For example, in an adult correctional center, preteens could help out in the reception area when visitors come in with small children who need to be cared for or entertained during the visit.

~ If you are concerned about confidential material, or "delicate business," let kids participate in indirect activities such as general maintenance, delivery, sorting supplies, etc.

~ Acknowledge the time required to prepare and supervise youngsters, but describe your ideas for alleviating some of this burden on the staff. (See the section "Supervision" later in this chapter.)

After all these issues have been examined, it may also be a good idea to schedule training sessions to help employees become more comfortable in working with children as volunteers.

One important suggestion is to start small. It is good management practice to pilot test any new idea and this one is no exception. Once administrators and staff understand that only a few children will be recruited at the beginning, they will be more open to giving the project a chance. You might also set a date to evaluate initial progress and get everyone's feedback.

Do not forget that adult volunteers presently on board will also be affected by the new presence of children. Enlist these veterans' aid in generating ideas for tasks that could be done by the youngsters and for many of the nitty-gritty implementation details. Give them a role in welcoming and supporting the boys and girls as co-workers.

Input from Children

The first way you might want to involve children is as advisors to you! Talk with children and get their opinions and ideas. These young advisors can be recruited from any source—including relatives of the salaried and volunteer staff—even if these initial young participants do not later become long-term volunteers.

You could arrange a "think tank" session, inviting five to ten youngsters to brainstorm with you about ways children could become volunteers with your program. Structure the discussion enough to remain focused, but create a comfortable, informal atmosphere so ideas will flow. Start by having the children contribute ideas on how needs of the agency might *generally* be met. Then select a few of these suggestions and examine each more closely, this time specifying: "how could kids help with these solutions?" Close by asking the think tank what training or preparation children might need to do the suggested jobs—and how a recruiting campaign might be implemented.

How to Run a "Think Tank"

Children Considering What Children Can Do

Why: To ask children themselves what young volunteers might be able to do to solve a problem or help your organization.

Who: At least five but not more than ten youngsters at one time. Works best if their age range is similar, no more than a three-year spread between the oldest and youngest. This way the group members share similar perspectives and respect one another's input. It is helpful if at least some of the children already know one another.

Time: 60 to 90 minutes, depending on the number of participants and their age (attention span).

Needs: A quiet, comfortable seating area (can be pillows on the floor). Avoid external interruptions.

A flipchart or blackboard, marking pens, masking tape; nametag materials.

Thirty (30) prepared squares of paper or index cards. Place a dollar sign on ten of the squares; draw "people" (stick figures are fine) on another ten. Leave the last ten blank.

Instructions:

1. If the children do not already know one another, do an ice breaker that introduces them. Have them make nametags for themselves.

2. Briefly describe either: a problem in the community that needs to be solved (who is affected by it, how it came about, what is already being done); or what your organization does, the people it helps, and the needs it meets. Give the children a chance to ask questions about the problem or about your organization.

3. Once you feel the group understands the need to be addressed, ask the children to think of ideas about how people might help—anybody, of any age. List these ideas on the flipchart or blackboard. Allow the ideas to flow without commenting on them (this is "brainstorming"). Write down every idea, no matter how it sounds to you at first.

4. When the children run out of ideas (allow time for silence before you assume they're done), discuss the list with them. Select those that seem to be the best ideas and star them.

5. Now put the prepared squares of paper on the table. Ask the children: "What is needed to make these ideas work?" Have them tape the dollar sign squares next to those that require some money and the people squares next to those that need volunteers. Use the blank squares for identifying other needs: donated materials, supplies, etc.

6. Now pose the following question: "How could kids help with these ideas?" Go through each of the selected ideas one at a time and list how youngsters could participate.

7. Finally, ask: "If kids were volunteers in this way, what would they need in order to do the job right?" Discuss what children would have to know (training), how they would have to be supported by adults (supervision), and what supplies or tools they would need.

8. Thank everyone for their help. Ask if anyone in the Think Tank wants to spend more time with you filling in the details of the ideas just listed.

"Brainstorming," in one form or another, is a technique familiar to many children. They will enjoy doing it with you because you have real-life questions to pose. Even if every idea generated is not workable, the think tank is a fun way to introduce you to the concept of collaborating with children. For detailed instructions on conducting a think tank, see the previous page.

Designing Assignments for Children

The examples in Chapter 3 of things youngsters have actually done as volunteers should prove that children can participate in almost any field of work. Your task is to determine what form such participation will take in your setting—which specific activities will benefit both your organization and the child. Remember that there are few concrete rules for involving children. You have to be willing to experiment to discover what works best for you. However, based on the opinions of childhood development specialists and of the directors of volunteers with experience in this area, there are some general guidelines to keep in mind when defining roles for young volunteers:

~ Beware of the myth that children will do anything "because they're young." The best jobs are ones children want to do.

~ Avoid sexist stereotyping. Assign work based on the interests of each child, rather than on some preconceived notions such as "boys like to work with their hands" or "girls don't like to get dirty."

~ Children often have fewer prejudices than adults. Use this open-mindedness to create cross-cultural, intergenerational, or interracial assignments. Though initially children may need preparation in facing a new situation (seeing a person in a wheelchair, hearing someone speak with an accent), they overcome such superficial barriers more quickly than adults.

~ On the other hand, children adopt the prejudices they hear expressed at home and may amaze you with their "opinions" on a variety of subjects. Therefore, do not assume open-mindedness and provide training before making a potentially embarrassing assignment. Children say what's on their minds.

~ Ask yourself, "what will the child get from this volunteer assignment?" Children volunteer for many of the same reasons adults do, so develop jobs that build on motivations such as learning something new, feeling important, and being of real help.

~ At the same time, your desire to provide a "good experience" for young volunteers should not overshadow your responsibilities to your clients/consumers. So also ask yourself, "does this job meet a real need?" This must be the bottom line question.

~ Children need to see immediate results, even on a small scale. Define assignments as a series of short-term tasks with identifiable goals or projects. This can be as simple as saying "today your job is to play checkers with Mr. Jones," or "please pick up the litter in this area." One of the most effective techniques to keep children motivated is to give them a sense of accomplishment.

~ Plan for some variety within each assignment. This will allow you to accommodate the physical, mental and emotional levels of different children. Offering assorted activities also keeps youngsters from getting bored and lets them choose what they really feel like doing at any given time. Attention span will vary with each child's age and maturity (and the nature of the task)—another reason for offering options.

~ Caution: too much freedom of choice is not necessarily productive. Children need a certain amount of structure. Find the happy medium between the extremes of "what do you want to do today?" and "this is what you will do today." Offering a choice between two or three tasks is probably ideal.

~ In designing jobs, identify whether literacy is needed to accomplish goals and, if so, what reading level is required. This is an important clue to which child can do the job.

Writing Job Descriptions

All the elements of an adult volunteer job description are appropriate for children, but the language and format should be less formal. Here are some suggestions for modifying the "official" tone of your job descriptions. Be careful, of course, not to use the same approach for pre-teens as you do for younger volunteers. Try:

~ simple language (and make it personal)

~ colored paper

~ large print (use special computer fonts, photocopiers that enlarge, or printshops that "blow up" a regularly-typed sheet; or find access to a large-print type-writer—try an elementary school or agency for the visually impaired)

~ graphics or illustrations

The way in which you word the information is important. Try a series of questions and answers, such as in the "Junior Reporter" job description on the next page.

> "They say that they have to shorten library hours and charge non-resident fees, so I volunteer. But they treat me like a baby. I really want to help and am able to, if they'd let me... I said that I would be willing to work at the front desk, but they stuck me upstairs, making signs. Some days I just sat around and did nothing, because I had nothing to do."
>
> —Lee Gilmore, age 12, Denver, CO

Write a job description for every assignment, even if the job is very simple or will be done by children who cannot read. The job description is a tool for you to pinpoint exactly what you want to have happen. Once you have a written job description, you can then explain the assignment orally to the non-literate child. You can even ask a young person who is able to read to present the job to the younger child.

When developing job descriptions for adult/child teams, do not fall into the trap of writing a single job description aimed at the adult. The child needs her/his own version. This is your first chance to demonstrate your expectation that the child will be a fully-contributing partner in the work.

When children volunteer in a group, their job descriptions should include something about what the group, as a whole, will accomplish as well as specific tasks to be done by each child individually.

Junior Reporter

What is this Job?

A Junior Reporter helps find news for the agency newsletter.

What will you do as a Junior Reporter?
· Talk to the Editor about a news story
· Make a list of questions for an interview
· Meet with people to get information
· Help to write short stories about what people said

Who is in charge?
You will be working with the Editor (Ms. Quincy). She will answer your questions and help you with your job.

Where will you work?
After talking to people all over the building, your desk for planning and writing will be in the Public Relations Office (Room 117).

How much time will this take?
We need you here once per week for two hours. The newsletter comes out once a month and you have the chance to write a story for each issue.

Who can do this job?
YOU can be a Junior Reporter if you:
· like to talk to people
· can write stories
· want to help the Editor with her work
· want to learn about being a reporter

Preparing for Special Needs

Transportation

Meeting transportation needs is a critical aspect of encouraging young volunteers who often do not have independent mobility. Getting to the work site might be especially difficult for children volunteering individually. Explore ways to provide rides or to reimburse bus fare. A small fundraiser may generate enough cash to provide young volunteers with money for public transportation.

Listed below are methods others have used. If you see an appropriate solution, give it a try. Or maybe this list can be a springboard for your own creativity.

~ car pool with adult volunteers

~ assign young volunteers to work off-site, in their own neighborhoods

~ use school buses (maybe get funding from special grants)

~ ask parents to be responsible for driving

~ use available chapter or organization vehicles

~ recruit from the immediate area so that youngsters can walk

~ transport your clients to where the children are

~ recruit assistance from a nearby corporation, senior center, church, or civic program

Work Space

Stock up on chair cushions! The smallest volunteers may need such adjustments in chair height to reach available work surfaces. If you plan on continuous involvement of young children as volunteers you might even want to invest in a set of small tables and chairs. But remember that many children are comfortable using the floor as a work space—a clean rug and some pillows might do the trick.

Children need more square feet of space than adults. Anticipate this need for elbow room and avoid assigning children to cramped areas.

It is ideal to provide children with a regularly-assigned work space. This minimizes insecurity by offering familiar surroundings from week to week.

As with any volunteer, it is a nice touch to have individual storage areas (cubbyholes, boxes, shelves, folders, etc.) in which the child can place his or her materials between visits. This also means setting aside a spot for children to leave their school books, coats, etc. while "on the job."

Refreshments

If you already provide some sort of refreshments for adult volunteers, expand the choice to include beverages appropriate for children. Something as simple as access to a water cooler can meet this need, especially if you keep flat-bottomed paper cups on hand so that the youngsters can bring the water back to their work sites. Boys and girls need beverages more frequently than adults, in order to maintain energy and concentration. Therefore, if you do not now offer drinks to volunteers, it is important to find a way to do so for children.

The need for refreshments varies somewhat with the time of day. Youngsters volunteering directly after school may need a snack as well as a beverage. If your facility relies on vending machines, be sure they are stocked with appropriate snacks and items such as juice. Alert parents to the need to supply children with coins for the machine, or make petty cash available for this purpose.

Your Building

Assess whether it will be hard for children to find or enter the restroom facilities currently used by adult volunteers. Be sure the restrooms are located as close as possible to the children's work sites.

Keep in mind that very young children may not be able to operate an elevator alone. Also, if your facility is large and maze-like, you may need to develop an escort plan to help the young volunteers find their way at first. The initial volunteers might produce a map for the next group of children.

Recruitment

The fundamentals of effective volunteer recruitment apply to children as well as adults: clear job descriptions; enthusiastic presentation; targeted approach according to skills needed; techniques chosen to match different audiences. There are three major sectors from which you can recruit children: schools, youth organizations, and the general public.

Schools

A growing number of public and private schools are appointing a "community service coordinator" (titles vary) to manage service-learning projects. In some cases the designated person is a full-time teacher who has accepted this added responsibility; in other cases a new staff member may be brought on board. If you can find such a coordinator, your recruitment task is much easier! This person will welcome your interest in placing students in your agency, particularly if the school has a service-learning program or requirement.

If you are approaching a school without a designated community service coordinator, you have some options. You can make your initial contact with the principal or with an individual classroom teacher. Almost any teacher is a possibility—service-learning can be connected to any grade or subject. Guidance counselors, school librarians, even the school nurse might be entry points.

Schools might also be tapped through the parent/teacher association or through existing extra-curricular clubs. Even the soccer team might be attracted to a special project.

Interestingly, our survey of children revealed some pluses and minuses to approaching them through school to volunteer. Advantages, from their point of view, included: it would make school more interesting; it would connect to classroom curricula; it could be done with classmates; it would "get us out of class"(!).

On the other hand, our young respondents saw some disadvantages to being recruited at school: they might feel pressured by their teachers; they are "already doing a lot" to help out in the school itself; anything connected to school is a "turn off'" for some youngsters.

Youth Organizations

Youth organizations are probably the best source for involving children in groups and are often seeking service projects for their youngsters. While some will welcome your new ideas, be aware that others are inundated with requests for assistance from community agencies. So you will be most successful if there is a clear match between your project and the type of group you approach.

The most visible organizations include Girl Scouts, Boy Scouts, 4-H, Campfire, etc. But think beyond these. Consider church/synagogue/mosque youth programs, sports leagues, special interest clubs, recreation centers, performing arts troupes, and after-school daycare. How about the juvenile justice system? Public housing projects? Don't forget to include resources such as summer camps if you have seasonal projects. All of these have adult leaders as contact points.

General Public

Up to here, we have suggested ways to contact children who are already organized under adult leaders. But children might want to volunteer for you as individuals or with their families. In this case, a parent or guardian must give permission for the child to volunteer. This means that all recruitment methods must address the double audience of children and parents.

The risk in recognizing the importance of parental permission is a tendency to concentrate attention on "selling" adults. While it is certainly appropriate to identify potential young volunteers through their parents, in the last analysis the child is the volunteer.

Occasionally, adults might view volunteering as a convenient form of "day care" for their children, especially after school or in the summer, when the search is on to keep youngsters occupied and out of trouble. You might even be pressured by staff or board members to accept their children for this purpose. So it is important to recruit children directly as much as possible. If a child is referred to you by an adult relative, do not assume that the child automatically understands or wants to participate.

Ask yourself where children can be found. Sources to tap include: video game arcades; record stores; playgrounds; Saturday matinees—be creative!

There are still other possible sources of young volunteers to consider including in your recruitment campaign:

~ The children or grandchildren (or nieces, nephews, cousins, etc.!) of staff members, present adult volunteers, and other adults connected with your organization

~The children of service recipients (present and past)

~ Younger siblings of present teenage or college-age volunteers

~ Siblings (younger or older) of clients, if your agency serves infants and/or youth

Finding Families

It should not be difficult to develop a recruitment campaign to encourage families to volunteer together. Remember: parents are always trying to spend quality time with their children. Volunteering is an ideal way to do that! The opportunity to spend more time together is especially appealing to working parents and to divorced parents living out of the home who want to do things with the children from whom they are separated. Volunteering as a family unit is a largely-undiscovered way for a parent and child to become better acquainted, share a common experience, and have "regularly-scheduled fun"!

So ask yourself: "Where can I find *parents*?" Some obvious answers include: parent/teacher associations; pediatricians' offices; children's clothing and toy stores; single parent support groups; spectator and audience sections of youth sports and performing arts events; marriage and divorce counseling services; schools and daycare centers at opening and closing times; parenting classes. Your recruiting materials can offer volunteer opportunities for families together and also for the children by themselves.

When your goal is to have parents encourage their children to volunteer, you might emphasize the benefits to their child such as: developing self-confidence; increasing maturity; exposure to new situations and types of people; constructive activity; and learning new skills.

Promotional Techniques

Depending on your community's acceptance of the idea of children as volunteers, you may need to begin by generating an awareness of the concept among the general public. This can be done collaboratively with other agencies and organizations. Consider enlisting the help of the social studies or civics department in your school system to incorporate volunteerism into lesson plans at all grade levels. This way children will begin to understand the difference between volunteering and working for pay.

Contact whatever local resources exist to help place prospective adult volunteers to see if they can help find children. Sources may include the Volunteer Center, American Red Cross, or the United Way.

A group of organizations might conduct a community volunteer "fair" emphasizing the roles children can play as volunteers. Bumper stickers, tee-shirts and billboards can be used to convey a sense of enthusiasm about the concept. Local radio and television stations might be enticed to help in publicity. Public access television now offers you the chance to highlight your search for young volunteers. If the kids tune in for tomorrow's school lunch menu, maybe they'll catch your recruitment message, too! And, don't forget the many new volunteer recruitment Web sites on the Internet.

When it comes to recruiting for your specific program, you will naturally select techniques that best match each source of potential volunteers. Our survey confirmed that youngsters respond especially well to brightly-colored posters, since this is a familiar form of communication in schools. The respondents also came up with some creative ideas, including messages on milk cartons (a real possibility if you have one local dairy), announcements in movie theaters, and TV/radio commercials.

The bottom line, however, is to find some personal way of asking each child to become involved. Chances are children will respond positively to a direct, face-to-face appeal, and are less likely to initiate a call to you even if they liked a poster or ad they saw.

Note that our young survey respondents repeatedly expressed a preference for ads and announcements in which *children themselves* deliver the message. So ask youngsters who are already volunteering to help recruit their peers.

Technology

Recruitment techniques must adapt to the times and in today's world the Internet is a major communication tool. There are several types of Web sites that can help you recruit young volunteers. First, there are volunteer opportunity registries that allow organizations—at no charge—to post their needs for volunteers. You can usually indicate an age range, whether or not families can volunteer together, and other relevant information. For the most updated list of such online registries, go to the Energize Web site at http://www.energizeinc.com/prof/volop.html.

> ## A Special Word to Those of You in All-Volunteer Groups
>
> The time has come to recognize that the children of your members are probably already contributing their efforts to the success of your program. How often have sons and daughters stuffed envelopes, distributed flyers, worked at bazaars, run errands, loaded cars, sold tickets, babysat for younger siblings, or rearranged their schedules to allow for members' meetings and phone calls?! Consider how you can build upon this corps of helpers and core of energy by involving these children officially. This means offering them choices as to assignment (maybe they would prefer the variety of helping other members of your organization, rather than always helping their own parents) and publicly thanking the youngsters for their good work.

There are also countless Web sites aimed at young people or at parents, many of which present volunteering or community service as a valuable activity. See if any such sites allow you to post messages or events.

For more information on using Internet technology in your recruitment campaign, see *The Volunteer Recruitment Book,* 3rd edition, by Susan J. Ellis (Energize, 2002).

Teacher/Group Leader Role

Since community service has already been incorporated into so many schools, teachers may be calling on you sooner than you think to place their students as volunteers in your agency. Even if the majority of your young volunteers come from youth organizations, there will undoubtedly be an adult leader with whom you will be dealing.

Schedule a meeting to clarify the expectations of the referring group and the role of the affiliated adult leader. A "roles and responsibilities" sheet with clearly delineated descriptions of who does what might be an initial goal to work on collaboratively. Reach agreement on such points as:

~ Who will obtain parental permission and generally liaison with parents?

~ Who will keep track of and follow up on children's absences?

~ How will responsibility for training and supervision be divided equitably and effectively between you?

~ What kinds of records will each of you need to keep?

~ Will the students receive any classroom "academic credit" for their volunteering? What is needed from you to document their learning for this?

~ How will you work together to enforce agency rules?

~ How will you keep in touch with each other?

~ Who is responsible for transportation of the young volunteers?

~ Who is responsible for insurance?

~ When is it appropriate to evaluate the work? When and how will this be done?

~ Will there be an end date to the project or continuous coverage by a new class of volunteers?

Discussing such questions at the beginning will avoid confusing duplication of roles and will establish good working relationships.

Be aware that teachers and group leaders may have unrealistic expectations of what your agency can offer young volunteers. Listen to their requests, but feel free to set limits on what will be possible. Your bottom line is service to your clients or consumers. For example, if a teacher wants students to "rotate" assignments every week so that they can observe agency operations, you can point out that this arrangement will not produce increased service. Find a compromise.

Interviewing and Screening

All the reasons to interview and screen adult volunteers operate for children as well, but there are four primary elements requiring special attention:

Choice: It is critical to determine whether the child really wants to volunteer. This may mean speaking with the child separately from his or her parent, or speaking individually with each member of a group of children who have been "volunteered" to help.

Job Description: The interview is the place to clarify—and, if necessary, to modify—the volunteer job description. Be sure the child understands your expectations and try to elicit her or his input. One good way to test understanding of the job description is to ask: "Now can you tell me in your own words what you'll be doing in this job?"

Literacy: You have the right to determine the reading and writing ability of each child old enough to be literate. Since grade level is not necessarily a reliable indicator, you may want to incorporate some reading and writing into the interview. This is a good reason to develop an application form. First of all, if you have an application form for prospective adult volunteers, you should have a parallel form for children. Second, this will allow you to test spelling, reading comprehension, neatness, etc.

Parental Permission: If a parent or guardian is present at the interview, by all means use this opportunity to obtain written permission and to answer any questions. (See Chapter 6 for more details about parental consent.) Mutually agree on an initial schedule for the child. If you do not meet the parent right away, some direct communication is important, beyond simply sending home a letter and form to be signed. A telephone call will insure that there are no misunderstandings and paves the way for future contact.

You might develop a "parent data sheet" as a companion to the child's application form to provide important information such as emergency contacts, telephone numbers and family insurance coverage. Also, you can note the transportation arrangement for the child that the parent has approved, so that you can be sure it happens as planned—catching the bus, meeting a relative, etc.

If you know that the child's volunteering is meant to be classroom related, use the interview to discuss what the child wants to learn from the experience with your organization. Are there any specific learning goals or requirements? Are there any skills the youngster wants to develop?

You are probably already a great interviewer of prospective volunteers, but we found a particularly good list of questions to ask children in the *VYTAL Manual*. We are sharing it with you on the next page.

It is possible that you will not want to accept every young applicant. Be aware that children are used to being told "no"—it is their parents who will have difficulty understanding why their child has been turned down! You can prevent some bad feelings by being careful not to imply that all applicants will automatically be accepted; mention the screening process during your recruitment.

When you are at the point of having to say no, try to focus on the needs of your agency, rather than on any shortcomings of the child (e.g., "We need someone who likes to paint," or "We need someone who can read without assistance"). Leave the door open for re-applying at a later date, since most of the time you will be rejecting a child because of developmental reasons, which can be outgrown. Be sure to encourage both parent and child to seek volunteer involvement elsewhere.

Even if the child has been referred to you by a school or court program requiring community service, you still have the right to refuse any volunteer applicant. It is not your organization's duty to fulfill an individual youngster's mandated service.

Discovering Yourself
How Will I Serve?

List #1	List #2

List #1

- Do you have special hobbies:?

- Do you have favorite sports?

- Have you learned to do anything special or different in the past year?

- If so, did you like learning how to do it? Are you any better at it now than when you started?

- Have you volunteered before?

- If so, did you like volunteering?

- Have you met any new people when you volunteered or when you were working at your hobbies?

- Did you enjoy talking to them?

- Do you think you might want to volunteer in the future?

- Are any of your friends volunteering now?

- Do they like it?

List #2

- What would you do with a free afternoon, if you could pick anything at all?

- Of all your hobbies, which do you like best?

- Why do you like that hobby best?

- How did you get interested in that hobby?

- Of any sports you play or watch which do you like best? Tell me what you like most about that sport.

- Who would you most like to talk to if you could pick anyone at all?

- What types of volunteering have you done in the past, if any?

- What kinds of volunteer activities do your friends do?

- How did they get started in these activities?

- Describe your most favorite vacation.

- Who went on that vacation with you?

- Why did you like that one the best?

Figure 2: This page has been reproduced with permission from the *VYTAL Manual*, Volunteer Action Center, United Way of Allegheny County, 200 Ross Street, Pittsburgh, PA, copyright 1989, p. 48.

Scheduling

It is most effective to schedule children in time slots of not more than three hours and probably an average of two hours at one time. Age, capabilities, and attention span will be the determining factors.

Children are "available" any time they are not in school, though it is possible to arrange for some involvement during school hours if this is a class project. While employed adults are often protective of their weekends and vacation periods, children frequently seek activities during these very times. Do not assume that late afternoons are always the best for children, since these hours are often filled already with music lessons, sports practices, and various and sundry appointments. Be open to creating ways for boys and girls to participate during weekend hours, even if this requires some special supervision plans.

Recognize that youngsters are not completely free to choose their volunteer schedule on their own. Parents must be consulted to avoid schedule conflicts and assure transportation. Also, there are seasonal changes in children's availability; school holidays, visiting relatives, family vacations, or exam periods can increase or decrease the time that can be committed to volunteering in a particular month. Therefore, it is probably advisable to confirm a child's volunteer schedule periodically with both parent and child so that temporary changes will not come as a surprise. This can work to your advantage by encouraging youngsters to give additional time during vacation periods.

Orientation and Training

The challenge of orienting and training young volunteers is to convey all the necessary information in a way that can be absorbed by young minds. Teaching children is a specialty and you may not feel qualified or comfortable doing this alone. Recruit adult volunteers with teaching skills to assist in designing training for the children who will volunteer.

Techniques for appropriate orientation and training include:

~ **Small Groups:** Try to limit the size of the trainee group to not more than ten, to encourage participation and to help you get to know each child.

~ **Visual Aids:** The more the better. Most children cannot sit through long speeches without things to look at. You can use illustrative posters, cartoons, puppets, slides, and videotapes. Hands-on items are wonderful for helping children understand reality. Being allowed to touch and sit in a wheelchair for example, teaches more than words or even pictures can convey.

~ **Handouts and Worksheets:** These are concrete tools to expand on information just presented. Boys and girls can work in small groups to complete such exercises. Again, remember to use large print and simple vocabulary.

~ **Tour of Facility:** Take a leisurely tour. Allow time for the children to satisfy their curiosity fully, both by peering into corners and by asking questions. Introduce each area as you approach it, but before you enter it. While still in the hall, prepare children for what they are about to see. Then enter the area and encourage exploration when possible.

One tip is to give the children some specific objects or activities to look for in each area. This could be done by giving out a sheet of pictures depicting things they will see during the tour (see sample below). This will keep them intrigued and will turn the tour into a learning game. Use your imagination. (If your building is large, you might consider scheduling several short tours over a period of weeks, rather than one overwhelmingly long one.)

~ **Work Areas:** Spend extra time showing the areas in which the children will work. Point out places to sit, store materials, etc. Show the rest rooms.

~ **Guest Speakers:** Invite other staff or volunteers, clients, etc. to speak to the children as appropriate.

~ **Buddy System:** Once oriented, each new child can be paired for a while with a child already experienced in the job to be done. This recognizes the ability of the "veteran" volunteers while providing a comfortable way for the newcomers to begin.

A different option when you are working with children in an organized group is to bring the orientation to them, off-site. This allows you to speak to all members of the class or group at once, rather than to be burdened with time-consuming repetition for each shift. It may be less intimidating to hear you on familiar ground before venturing into your facility. Also, the youngsters may be doing a project away from your agency and so do not need to come on site.

You will, of course, determine the content of your orientation and training program based on the nature of the work to be done. Balance general information with specific job instructions. The age and skills of the children, plus the difficulty of their assignments, will determine your training plan.

The training period is the time to emphasize your expectations about work habits, some of which may be new to young volunteers. Go over such basics as proper dress, attendance, punctuality, and appropriate behavior. You should discuss what a "supervisor" is and how a young volunteer can get help with a question or problem. This same information should be conveyed to the parents or adult leader as well, since they need to understand what you expect from their children.

One concern in your organization might be confidentiality. If young volunteers will have access to private records, you might want to set aside specific time to emphasize the importance of confidentiality. Depending on the age of the children, using examples relevant to their own lives is one way to underscore the importance of honoring privacy. You can assure youngsters that you would not have allowed them to volunteer in your agency if you did not think you could trust them. Nevertheless, you must emphasize this important issue. It might be helpful to include examples of the potential consequences of breaking confidentiality accidentally or acting on information obtained as privileged information.

Supervision

Your supervisory responsibilities will vary depending upon which type of management you select for the children's project. Your choices are:

~ *You* supervise the children directly.

~ *Another employee* supervises the children.

~ An *adult teacher* or *group leader* acts as supervisor on site.

~ The *adult* or *teenage volunteer* team member supervises the child to whom s/he is matched.

~ An *adult volunteer* supervises the entire children's project.

Supervision is what makes the project function day to day. The supervisor must: give instructions; prepare work; plan for manageable sequence of tasks; provide encouragement; reinforce success; troubleshoot; and recognize accomplishments. Just keep in mind that you must prepare anyone responsible for supervising the young volunteers—do not assume willingness or ability. Training of staff and adult volunteers will probably be necessary to assure that children will be welcomed and supported.

Any supervisor of young volunteers should like children and feel comfortable around them. This will help a lot, especially because youngsters are sensitive to the attitudes of adults. Success in working with children relies more on an innate "sixth sense" than on hard-and-fast rules. Certainly there should be policies and procedures, but be open to the unexpected. Remember that one of the main reasons you recruited youngsters is to benefit from their fresh approach and creativity, so do not squelch the potential.

The age of the children involved will dictate the style of supervision to a large extent. For example, one program administrator shared this thought about supervising volunteers ages nine to fourteen:

I...encourage the young people to assess their limits and be able to say "halt" when they're getting in over their heads. They seem reluctant to express this and then begin to fall by the wayside. I try to head this off by talking with them periodically, encouraging them to keep up to date with me and with themselves about their needs, likes, dislikes, etc.[2]

Youngsters are able to evaluate how their assignments are working out. Continuous mutual assessment will keep things on the right track.

Adult supervisors will find themselves acting as "teachers" when supervising young volunteers. This is natural and positive. Volunteering is a learning experience for everyone, but this is more pronounced for children. The teaching occurs, not with a "lesson plan," but through questions and answers tangential to the task at hand. Children need to have their work placed into the broader context, which is usually new to them.

Older children can be given substantial independent responsibility once they are trained and accustomed to their assignments. They can sign themselves in, get their own supplies, and do their jobs even when their immediate supervisor is not available. This means that children can volunteer on weekends, when the regular staff is not on duty. The youngsters and the agency should know who is in charge if a question arises, but constant supervision may not be necessary.

Recognition

If adult volunteers in your facility wear uniforms, badges, or have an identification card, provide something similar for the children. Nametags might be a nice touch for the boys and girls, even if not worn by anyone else.

Keep the same records of attendance and activities done by the children as you do for adult volunteers. It may not be necessary to be concerned with written progress reports from the youngsters, but it is important to establish some type of regular communication system to monitor progress.

Simple feedback forms, short group meetings, and informal conversations can all be used to help you stay informed about how the volunteer work is going and to help each child reflect on the experience.

Don't forget that, as with adult volunteers, it is a form of recognition to ask for and consider seriously the child's opinions about your organization.

Consider ways to thank each child publicly within peer group settings and via school and community newspapers, church/synagogue bulletins, etc. Children love parties, so recognition "events" can be fun, comparatively inexpensive (cookies, cake, punch), and easy to organize. Encourage the children to invite family members and friends to the party. These guests will learn more about how helpful the children are to your program and you might even be able to recruit some new volunteers.

One idea for a recognition gift is a specially-made button that the children can wear to proclaim their involvement as volunteers. The Parks and Recreation Service of Idaho gave a brightly-colored button saying "Junior Ranger" to each young volunteer who collected litter at park campsites. Such buttons are appealing as a tangible, immediate reward for work accomplished.

* * * * * * *

Having children aboard as volunteers is not necessarily more or less work than having adults as volunteers—but it is different in the ways just described. There are few shortcuts, but success is definitely attainable.

> "This positive experience was shared by the youth as well as the residents. Prior to the shopping trip, I presented an extensive orientation to prepare the children for what was expected of them and what the residents were like. There was an excellent response by the children. They felt in control at the mall because they were responsible. This project was a stimulus for future volunteer projects for youth in our facility."
>
> —Beverly Evans, Director of Volunteers, The Virginia Home, Richmond, VA, who organized a shopping mall expedition for disabled adult residents escorted by 10 to 12-year-olds from a nearby vacation Bible school.

---

[2] Rev. Marsha L. B. Irmer, Director of Volunteer Services, Lutheran Nursing Home, Brockton, Massachusetts, in a letter to Energize, January 1982.

(Especially for teachers and other leaders of children, but worthwhile for leaders of volunteer programs, too.)

The preceding chapter speaks to the organizational director of volunteers who is interested in finding and utilizing young volunteers. This chapter, on the other hand, is for those of you who already have responsibility for a group of children and are seeking ways to help them serve the community.

Choosing What to Do

There are no limits to what your group can do—volunteers are active in every aspect of community life. One of the basic premises of a democracy is that any citizen, of any age, can identify a need or problem and go to work on it. Therefore, you can encourage your children to determine the things about which they are most concerned and show them that they have the power to do something about these. Even if there is no ready-made formal opportunity for addressing an identified need, the children can proceed on their own if you are willing to provide leadership. So start by deciding jointly what you all want to do. Take a look at Chapter 3 to jump-start your thinking.

It may not be easy at first to select a volunteer project, even if you are under a mandate to do so because of a requirement in the school curriculum. The children may need some orientation to the concept of "volunteering" in general and may need time to explore the many areas in which they can help. There is a growing number of service-learning curricula available for various grade levels that provide exercises and discussion guides for your use. Several are listed in the Resource section at the end of this book.

In addition, on page 31, we describe a "think tank" session that could be used as a technique for stimulating actual project ideas and options. Be careful not to limit creativity because of prior expectations—just because your boys and girls took part in a bike-a-thon in the past does not necessarily mean they have to do the same thing again this year.

Everyone Benefits

Volunteer projects have a success record of dramatically making a difference in the lives of their young participants. The youngsters often improve their grades, gain self-esteem, learn problem-solving processes, form new relationships, and see themselves as members of a community.

This is especially the case if you are working with children who have been labeled "underachievers," "disabled," "disturbed," "at risk," or "delinquent." There are many examples of actual community service programs that have given these types of youngsters the chance to prove that they can be givers as well as recipients of service.

One can assume that you are already sold on the strengths and abilities of the children you lead. True, you know their limitations, but you also have continuous opportunity to see how much they can do. For example, some adults would be astonished at the capabilities of eight-year-olds, while you may have come to take their talents for granted. Be prepared to advocate for your group's talents.

Choice

The essence of volunteering is the element of choice. Children have few alternatives as to how they will spend their time. Usually an adult determines when they will learn geography, when they will go to dance class, and when they will go to bed. For youngsters, therefore, volunteering is a welcome opportunity to have some control over their own time and learning.

Sometimes children are forced into activities selected by "majority rule." While it is important for children to learn about democratic group process, it is equally important to stress the voluntary nature of volunteering. No child should be forced to participate in anything labeled "volunteer." This may mean having to develop a second project for the youngsters who do not wish to join the main group project, or finding individual volunteer assignments to match special interests.

Remember that even in a mandated, school-based community service program there is choice. Requiring a certain number of service hours for all students is not the same as predetermining the specific project or assignment for each individual child. Children should be able to choose the activities in which they most want to participate.

There is, however, a paradox which should be considered as you determine the options you plan to offer children: they cannot make a commitment to volunteer as an independent decision. Their "voluntary-ness" is ultimately subject to approval and logistical support from an adult authority (parent, teacher, etc.). Keeping this in mind, you can still provide opportunities for choice by offering a broad selection of service activities.

Options for Service

One factor in selecting what the children want to tackle is the amount of time they (and you) intend to commit.

Short-term or one-time projects allow for intensive involvement and immediate rewards that are, of necessity, limited in scope. Keep in mind that individual children who become very interested in a short-term project begun by the group can always elect to continue volunteering on their own.

Long-term or ongoing projects enable the group to affect more complex problems, but require continuous coordination and motivation. One approach to providing long-term service is to schedule other groups sequentially to pick up where your group left off.

Try using this exercise from the *VYTAL Manual* to help your children discover the many things volunteers do in your community.

INFLUENCING MILLIONS DAILY

VOLUNTEER NEWS

Write findings in space below

List any articles, ads, or announcements about volunteer group activities

---

Use any recent newspaper issue as a resource.

☐ ....
....

☐ ....
....

☐ ....
....

☐ ....
....

☐ ....
....

How do these activities help solve problems or meet needs?

Volunteers are hard at work in your community

The local newspaper is a great source of information about what volunteers are doing

---

List newspaper stories about individual volunteers and their work:

Why is the story newsworthy enough to be in the newspaper?

☐ ....

☐ ....

☐ ....

☐ ....

☐ ....

Figure 3: This page has been reproduced with permission from the *VYTAL Manual*, Volunteer Action Center, United Way of Allegheny County, 200 Ross Street, Pittsburgh, PA, copyright 1989, p. 142.

The next important decision to make is whether you will launch a project independently or whether you will link up with an already-established volunteer effort. Your decision will be determined by a number of considerations, including what agencies are in your area, the make-up of your group, and the specific activities that the children themselves most want to do.

Independent Projects

If you choose the route of a self-managed project not connected to any established community agency, be prepared to assume the role of "director of volunteers" as described in Chapter 4. This is not as overwhelming as it may seem at first glance, partly because you are probably doing a lot of coordinating already. Examine the steps outlined in Chapter 4 and adapt them to the way you presently work with the youngsters in your group.

One benefit of an independent project is that the children have maximum participation in determining the structure as well as the content of the volunteer work.

However, you may have to find outside resources to supplement the leadership you provide. This may mean experts, funds, materials, or facilities. In addition, a self-managed project may need publicity, clearance from authorities, or other arrangements to assure success.

In planning, be sure to determine specific goals and time frames carefully and realistically. There should be a clear product or ending point, so that the children feel the satisfaction of accomplishment. Define your role so that you are not overburdened with what could be a great deal of coordinating responsibility. Recruit other adults to assist in providing support.

One last idea: look for other youth groups sharing your youngsters' concerns. Collaborative community service projects increase the number of minds and hands at work, with the added bonus of providing an opportunity to cooperate with a new (and possibly diverse) group of children.

While the independent route may initially seem easier, there are many good reasons to consider joining forces with other volunteer efforts already underway. This avoids duplicating the efforts of others and reinventing procedures. Before plunging in on your own, find out what is going on in your community related to your group's interest—do not assume there is nothing already being done.

Linking with Existing Efforts

As you do some research, you may be surprised at the number and scope of established volunteer programs in your community. If you are lucky enough to have a Volunteer Center in your area, start there, or searc the Internet. Just about every type of nonprofit agency and many government departments have structured ways for adults to contribute voluntary service. Look beyond the obvious (hospitals or nursing homes) to volunteer programs in such settings as parks, museums, fire departments, courts, public radio stations, etc. Service projects may already be underway for older students in some of these agencies; perhaps these settings would be willing to consider younger children, too.

Apart from agencies and government offices, most all-volunteer organizations and associations sponsor projects involving their members. Such groups might also welcome the volunteer contributions of your youngsters. When you consider the wide range of public service performed by civic clubs, fraternal organizations, labor unions, professional societies, advocacy groups, tenant organizations, and social clubs, you can see that the interests of the children you lead probably coincide with something already being done.

Once you have located a potential agency or group to work with, you must then find the right contact person. Do not assume this will be the executive director or president. Start by asking if there is a "director of volunteers" or "volunteer coordinator." You are in luck if the answer is yes, since that person should be looking for offers of help. Not every agency has a full-time person in charge of volunteers, so you may end up working with people as diverse as curators, casework supervisors, community relations personnel, or activity directors. In the case of an all-volunteer group, you probably would work with an officer or committee chairperson.

On the other hand, you may be approached by an organization's representative seeking to recruit your group. As the concept of young volunteers gains acceptance, the most forward-thinking service providers will be reaching out to find willing youngsters.

By meeting with the contact person, you will be able to determine what your role in the project will be:

~ If the person is experienced and enthusiastic about all volunteers, you can expect her or him to proceed as outlined in Chapter 4. You will mainly have to provide back-up support.

~ If the person is reluctant to welcome volunteers as young as yours, you may need to convince the agency of the capabilities of children by discussing specific ways they can contribute. Suggest that s/he read this book!

~ If the person is enthusiastic, but inexperienced in volunteer management, you will need to collaborate on the responsibilities outlined in Chapter 4. This guidebook does not provide information on all the things necessary to work successfully with volunteers in general, so you may want to seek out other resources, as well.

~ Be sure to answer all the questions on page 40 jointly.

Since it is vital to have the complete endorsement of the person coordinating volunteers, if you cannot sell the idea of young volunteers to him or her, go somewhere else!

The benefit of finding a "home" for your group in an established program is clear: everything is already in place to support the children's activities. However, be certain that the interests of the children are really being met and that available volunteer assignments provide the opportunities you seek. Be realistic about what your children can do and understand that the primary concern of the organization will be to serve its clients, not your youngsters.

However, if you have to do too much compromising about how your group will be utilized, perhaps gaining the security of a formal agency or organization is not worth sacrificing the children's initial goals. Either find another agency or opt for doing an independent project.

Point Person

It is likely that more and more teachers in your school or group leaders in your organization will be arranging service projects with their youngsters. As time goes on, it will be more efficient to designate one "point person" to coordinate outreach to the community. The coordinator's primary role will be to identify willing and interesting placement sites for young volunteers. This avoids duplication of effort for all the adult leaders and decreases the number of contacts that agencies receive from your organization. Everybody wins.

"It's a bow tie, with the agency's needs on one side and the school's needs on the other and I'm the knot. Both the agency's needs and the school's needs have to be satisfied and it is up to the school coordinator to pull it all together."

—Stephanie Judson, Service Learning Coordinator and teacher of Religious Thought at Friends Select School in Philadelphia.

Legalities and Liabilities

There are lots of bug-a-boos about the legalities of involving children as volunteers, which can stop you in your tracks if you do not anticipate them. Legal questions are undoubtedly important to answer, but be aware that others may place the fear of liability in your path as an insurmountable obstacle. This tactic is often a smokescreen hiding greater resistance to the whole concept of involving children. Your counter-tactic is accurate information. Armed with the facts about law and insurance, you can prove that such issues do not have to stop the progress of your program.

This chapter is designed to get you started with some basic information. We had hoped to provide more definitive do's and don'ts, but soon realized that state laws vary too much to allow generalizing. There are few experts in the special area of volunteers and the law, so we had to hunt for and piece together the facts. The following sources contributed to our research in their particular subjects of expertise:

~ U.S.Department of Labor; Employment Standards Administration: Wage and Hour Division
~ Jeffrey D. Kahn, Esq.
~ Juvenile Law Center, Philadelphia, PA
~ University of Pennsylvania School of Law
~ Department of Insurance, American College, Bryn Mawr, PA
~ American Institute for Property and Casualty Underwriters
~ Volunteer Insurance Service Association
~ Prudential Insurance Company
~ Germantown Friends School, Philadelphia, PA
~ Lutheran Nursing Home, Brockton, MA
~ Virginia Office of Volunteerism

Here is what we learned....

Federal Child Labor Laws

The Federal child labor laws for the United States are contained in the Fair Labor Standards Act and regulations issued under the Act. (The Fair Labor Standards Act is also the law that sets minimum wage and overtime requirements). If you wish to read the child labor regulations for yourself, order Child Labor Bulletin No. 101 from the Wage and Hour Division of the U.S. Department of Labor or download it for free at <http://www.dol.gov/esa/regs/compliance/whd/childlabor101.pdf>.

You can also learn more from the Department of Labor Web site at <http://www.labor.gov/dol/topic/youthlabor/index.htm>, and the new (2002) Web site called "Youth Rules" at < http://www.youthrules.dol.gov/>. (The Internet puts such information at your fingertips in many other countries as well.)

The Fair Labor Standards Act only applies to employment regulations and does not apply to volunteers. According to WH Publication 1297 of the Wage and Hour Division (pages 6 and 7), volunteers are not covered by the Act because they do not receive monetary compensation.

Therefore, there is nothing in Federal child labor laws that expressly forbids or limits children under the age of fourteen from becoming *volunteers*. The issue of unsalaried work by children is actually not addressed at all. In a free society, we assume permission to do something if there is no specific law against it.

It is nevertheless worth noting the provisions of the Federal child labor laws. Except for clearly-defined exceptions, all employment of children under the age of fourteen is considered "oppressive child labor" and is illegal. Also illegal is the employment of young people under the age of eighteen in "hazardous" work. Very few would disagree with the definition of "hazardous" work, since it covers such activities as operating power equipment and handling explosives or dangerous substances. In some settings, "hazardous" work also specifically includes working on ladders and large-scale cooking. (Agricultural jobs are discussed in a separate set of regulations.)

It would be wise and prudent (and downright smart!) to design assignments for young volunteers in compliance with the general restrictions of child labor laws. After all, if a situation is considered hazardous for youth over age fourteen, it certainly would also be hazardous for a younger child.

For most of you, determining safe volunteer roles for children is not a problem. But some of you, notably those working with programs in parks and recreation departments, hospitals, disaster relief programs, etc., should double-check your youth volunteer assignments with legal counsel.

State or Licensing Regulations

As with everything else, labor laws differ from state to state. Check your state's definition of "employee" and "volunteer," age restrictions on employment, and description of "hazardous" work. But just because there are restrictions on the *employment* of children, do not automatically assume you cannot utilize youngsters as *volunteers*.

You need to look for supplements to and annotations of your state's child labor laws for any relevant applications to volunteering. For example, in Pennsylvania, the State Attorney General issued a ruling that specifically permits youth under age sixteen to volunteer in conservation and parks programs. Even if you find no such clear directives, as long as nothing *forbids* the volunteer work, you may assume a green light.

When a school district mandates a community-service requirement, it is obvious that a governmental authority is giving authorization for children to do volunteer work.

Questions to Ask

There are two main sources of information you need to contact to get a definitive answer on legal issues for your program: your State Department of Labor and your organization's lawyer. Ask the following basic question: Are there any legal restrictions on what children can do as volunteers in our state?

If applicable, you may also have to contact the state licensing or national accrediting authority for your agency (e.g., Department of Aging for a nursing home; Big Brothers/Big Sisters of America for a local chapter; etc.). Determine if there are any guidelines or actual regulations about utilizing children as volunteers. Do you need a parental consent form? For what, specifically, and how should the form be worded?

Beware, however, that the answers you receive may be based on *tradition* rather than fact. If you receive contradictory responses, pursue your questions further. Distinguish between *guidelines* and *regulations*—remember that the former are optional.

Find out from your lawyer when it is best to get answers to such questions in writing.

Insurance

Separate from questions of law is the issue of insurance coverage for young volunteers—a second bug-a-boo! In our litigious society, a common fear is that the organization will be held liable should a child be hurt while volunteering for it. Protection against costs connected to such risk is available. Of course, this issue is tied to the type and degree of insurance coverage already provided for both employees and adult volunteers.

While there are many kinds of problems to insure against, the most important ones to discuss here (for both the child and the agency) are: *a volunteer could get hurt;* and *someone else could get hurt as a result of something a volunteer does.*

The following are the categories of insurance that you will most likely need to consider. Our intention is to give you enough general information to enable you to pursue this subject intelligently, but we caution you that the following is by no means an in-depth analysis of insurance.

Liability Insurance protects the organization from financial loss by paying damages (up to the dollar value of the insurance policy) resulting from a claim, including the cost of any legal defense.

Personal Liability Insurance protects the individual volunteer in the same way.

Accident Insurance covers the cost of medical treatment (up to the dollar amount of the policy) required as the result of an accident. For volunteers, you will probably be exploring "Excess Accident Medical Coverage," which applies only to the actual times volunteers are working on your behalf and adds to any personal coverage they may already have.

Provision of such medical coverage does not prevent lawsuits (hence the need for liability insurance, as well), but past experience of insurance companies shows that the payment of expenses incurred after an accident often deters litigation. This is because the organization's willingness to cover costs is seen as a "goodwill gesture."

Workers' Compensation provides for economic recovery by an employee after a work-related injury, regardless of its cause. The coverage includes medical costs, lost earnings, rehabilitation expenses, and death benefits—in exchange for which the employee usually loses the right to sue the employer for negligence. So this system protects both parties. Workers' Compensation can be provided through a State agency or private insurance companies (in some cases, an organization may be "self-insured").

In some states, rulings have been made that permit certain categories of volunteers to be provided with Workers' Compensation coverage, recognizing the quasi-employee status of these "unpaid personnel." Even if your adult volunteers are presently covered under such a plan, in almost all cases volunteers under the age of fourteen will not be eligible. This is because Workers' Compensation is designed for those who are or "could" be salaried, and children cannot be employees. So you will probably have to seek special coverage for your youngest volunteers.

Once again, our research in this area made it very clear that insurance regulations and availability differ widely from state to state. The preceding categories are fairly standard, but you will need to obtain specific details for your own location.

Note that many children you recruit will be already covered by family insurance policies. If so, your concern is *excess* coverage and protection for special situations. However, you may encounter parents who do not want to use their own insurance to cover their children when volunteering, for whatever reason. If this is the case, "first dollar" coverage may be needed, again as a goodwill gesture. If the children serve as volunteers through an official school program, there is every likelihood that they will be covered by the school's insurance plan. In fact, if the service is mandated, you have every right to expect the school to pay attention to insurance questions. Youth organizations that commonly sponsor community involvement projects may also provide their own coverage. But do not make assumptions—ask who will be responsible for insurance.

Liability Waivers

A liability waiver is a form stipulating that the signer understands the possible risks of a situation and agrees to hold another party harmless in case of injury. Universal legal opinion, however, is that such documents do *not* protect against litigation (regardless of how carefully the form is worded). This is because a person can always claim that s/he did not fully understand the extent or nature of the risk. Further, though some waivers may state that the signer will not bring a lawsuit in any circumstance, situations may later arise in which the volunteer will be permitted to take legal action.

So why bother? First, the waiver provides an opportunity to discuss the potential risks of a situation in advance. Second, the signed waiver can be used in a lawsuit as evidence of your attempt to inform the person of her/his risk. Third, the waiver acts as a psychological deterrent in that many people will honor the agreement not to sue just because they have signed it.

Adult volunteers obviously can make their own decisions about risk and whether to sign a waiver. Minors, on the other hand, have no legal right to sign anything for themselves. So it is imperative that you obtain a parent's or guardian's signature on the liability waiver relating to the child.

The best liability waivers are the most specific. This may mean wording a different waiver for each risky volunteer assignment, or developing a waiver for each trip or event as it occurs. Blanket, general waivers are virtually useless because it is so easy for the signer to say later: "I didn't know that the waiver covered *that*."

For the record, it should be noted that courts go to great lengths to protect children and might even allow a person who has reached adult age to sue for damages incurred when s/he was a minor, even if his or her parents signed a liability waiver at the time. But this would have to be a very special case.

Parental Consent

Parents and guardians have many legal rights over their children. Therefore, you should consider whether or not parental consent must be obtained before a child can become an official volunteer. There are a few situations in which parental consent may be implied, such as activities occurring as part of the normal classroom day. But in other cases, parents/guardians should be informed of and agree to the volunteer activities of their children, at least as a courtesy.

Whether or not you obtain consent for legal reasons, the process of getting permission has value because it allows you to convey to parents the overall picture of their child's involvement in your program. Then the parent's signature is as much an acknowledgment of understanding as it is a sign of legal permission. On the next page is an actual consent form used by the Lutheran Nursing Home in Brockton, Massachusetts. Note the many pieces of information that are conveyed on this single sheet. This is only one model—design your own.

We further suggest that you attach a copy of the volunteer job description for the child's actual assignment. This makes it clear exactly what the consent is for. (It is not a bad idea to have a lawyer approve your wording.)

Another possibility is to combine the parental consent form with a liability waiver. See the example on the next page.

Protecting Children

The world has become a much scarier place since the earlier editions of this book, or at least the subjects of child abuse, pedophilia, and kidnapping have become common topics of discussion and media attention. In fact, in the United States we are close to panic about protecting children. Recent scandals regarding the sexual abuse of children by clergy have only fueled the fire.

Whether in paid employment or volunteering, most states now require an organization to conduct official background checks of any adult whose assignment involves working with minors in any way. This includes criminal records and child abuse reports. Legislation such as "Megan's Law" enable a community to keep track of those convicted of pedophilia. So, if you will be recruiting children as volunteers, you should research whether or not you must screen your staff or adult volunteers first.

Paranoia aside, everyone wants to keep children safe from harm. It is sensible to develop a risk management plan that protects everyone, the children from being abused and adults from being falsely accused. For example, limit twosomes. It's safer for everyone if there are at least two adults present when only one child is in the room, or several children present when there is only one adult.

There are many Web sites—for many countries—devoted to preventing child abuse and new online services that will conduct background checks for a fee. Naturally you

lutheran nursing home
mr. john g. magistrelli, administrator
888 north main street
brockton, ma 02401
617/587-6556

CONSENT FORM
YOUNG VOLUNTEERS PROGRAM

TO: The parent/s or guardian/s of:_____

From: Pastor Marsha L. B. Irmer, Director of Volunteer Services

    In order for your child to become a volunteer at the Lutheran Home,
we must receive your written consent. Please read and sign the attached
form; and, if you have questions or concerns, feel free to call me
weekdays at the Home between 9 a.m. and 3 p.m. You are also encouraged
to visit the Home if you have not already done so; and I will be happy to
arrange a tour for you.
    We appreciate your child's interest and concern in this important
area of health care. It will mean a great deal to our elderly residents
and to our staff.
    Thank you!

- -

CONSENT FORM
YOUNG VOLUNTEERS PROGRAM

I give my permission for _____to volunteer at
the Lutheran Nursing Home.

I understand that s/he:
          - is to participate in an Orientation/Training program prior to
            beginning volunteer service at the Home.
          - will work out a monthly schedule of volunteer hours with the
            Director of Volunteer Services (to also be checked with family
            schedules at home).
          - will be expected to comply with the "Guidelines for Volunteers"
            and to be faithful in honoring his/her volunteer commitment.

I also understand that, should s/he fail to comply with the Guidelines or
fail to keep a commitment without giving the Home adequate advance
notice, s/he will be on probation and will have to re-evaluate his/her
volunteer participation with the Director.

                    _____
                    (Signature & Date)

                    _____
                    (Your relationship to the Volunteer)

(Unless there are further questions, please detach this form and have
your child return it with his/her application. Thank you.)

should talk to your organization's lawyer, but do some research yourself to prepare. Start at the Nonprofit Risk Management Center <http://www.nonprofitrisk.org> which produces many excellent resources on preventing child abuse, volunteer management risks, and other relevant subjects.

Exploring Your Own Situation

The purpose of this entire section is to urge you to check out your own situation and get the type of protection appropriate for your organization and its young volunteers. In order to do a thorough job, you need to touch base with your agency's present insurance carrier(s) for employees and adult volunteers. You may start by contacting your agent(s) orally, but eventually you should obtain written answers to your questions from the legal department of the insurance company, to be sure you have an authoritative response to support you in case of need. Further, if Company A says a particular situation is covered by Company B's policy, make sure Company B agrees!

> "In giving leadership to young volunteers, as volunteers, I think we do a great deal more for the future of our society than with any other group because, after all, the people who are youth today are the ones who are going to be running this country before you know it. The way they feel about themselves and the way they feel about their ability to make a real difference is going to make the difference in whether this democratic society is going to survive or not."
>
> —Harriet H. Naylor, in a 1977 speech to the Child Welfare League of America

Don't stop there. Approach a sampling of other insurance companies that may be able to offer better and less expensive coverage for your situation. Remember that insurance is a business and that carriers can design any type of insurance for which someone is willing to pay. Some companies may have prior experience in covering groups of children in other settings and therefore can respond to your needs more easily (and at less cost). Perhaps you might talk to the company underwriting your local school system's insurance; companies that handle school policies are obviously already used to providing coverage for children.

You are exploring group coverage, traditionally the most cost-effective way to cover individuals. Group coverage allows for great flexibility in designing an insurance program, since each policy is written to match an organization's specific needs. Explore those agencies already offering policies for volunteer programs. We encourage you to feel confident in *negotiating* with insurance companies for the best coverage.

The following are the types of questions you should raise both with insurance companies and with your organization's lawyer:

~ Are children as volunteers included in our present insurance coverage? Are there any gaps in such coverage?

~ Do we need accident or excess accident insurance for children?

~ Do you see any of our assignments as especially risky for children?

~ Do we need a parental consent form? For what, specifically? How should the form be worded?

~ Do we need a liability waiver? For what, specifically? How should the form be worded?

~ Do we need to do any criminal or child abuse background checks on either employees or adult volunteers here?

~ What information should we get from parents about their family insurance policies?

~ Is family coverage sufficient in our case?

~ What if a child's family does not have coverage or prefers not to apply their coverage to our program?

~ Does it make a difference, in terms of agency liability, if parent and child volunteer together (and therefore the parent is with the child while at the agency)? How?

~ Is the personal liability of an adult volunteer affected if s/he is asked to supervise a young volunteer? What about the personal liability of salaried staff and the director of volunteers, if supervising children as volunteers?

Don't Worry!

We have presented this section in recognition that legal and insurance issues must be addressed by any good volunteer program. But if we have only succeeded in leaving you catatonic (!), then we have defeated our purpose. We want to give you confidence in dealing with lawyers and insurance agencies, and to show you that the situation is manageable. This should also enable you to respond effectively if your organization's administration challenges, on the basis of legalities, your intent to recruit youngsters.

Designing insurance coverage forces one to imagine the worst scenarios possible. The chances of such horrible things actually happening are very remote. Once you have taken the necessary precautions to protect the youngsters and your agency, **do not let fear limit you!** You are now free to focus on all the creative, upbeat aspects of managing a program involving children as volunteers.

> "Adults are afraid of looking like a fool...Kids could not care less. If you're not afraid to take a risk, to make mistakes, then more things are open to you."
>
> —George Moynihan, Assistant Director, Lawrence Hall of Science Computer Education Project

Families Together

(Especially for parents who want to explore volunteering as a family.)

From our experiences with the first edition of *Children as Volunteers*, we know that some parents are attracted to this book because they are intrigued by the idea of volunteering as a family activity. The preceding chapters have given you a perspective on the preparations agencies, schools, and youth organizations need to make in order to enable youngsters to volunteer. Not every setting will value the contributions of your children, but it is worth the effort to seek out those that do.

What do you gain by volunteering as a family? First of all, you capture that elusive but much wished for goal of "quality time" together. If you are already active as a volunteer in community agencies, you can continue your participation with less guilt about the time you spend away from your children. Now you'll be *with* them—and the organizations you care about receive even more help!

Group volunteering allows you to get to know your children in new ways, and vice versa. The process of demonstrating skills and learning new ones gives both age levels the chance to respect each other, share a common goal, and have something to talk about all week. It is an added benefit if you are also mixing teenage children with younger ones.

Selecting Your Family Project

The process of choosing what you want to do together follows much the same logic as what we suggested to the youth group leaders in Chapter 5. Do you want to volunteer as part of an established, formal volunteer program or do you want to do something independently? Will you join with other families on your block or in your church or synagogue, or is this an activity that you will value more if you do it alone? There are no set answers.

Also, there are many variations on the theme of family volunteering. It can mean every member of the family at the same time, doing the same thing. But other options include: going to a site together but then handling different work assignments and rejoining each other when you go home; accepting the responsibility for a particular project but having flexibility in whether all or some of you do it each week; one parent and one child as a twosome; involving extended family members such as grandparents, aunts and uncles, or cousins. For divorced, non-custodial parents, volunteering can be something special to share with your children instead of purely playtime during your visits.

Always remember that volunteering is something you all will be doing in your so-called leisure time. In other words, you will be squeezing it into your schedule among school and jobs, homework and yard work. The real "competition" will be between possible volunteer projects and other recreational opportunities...so make sure what you choose is fun to do. It certainly can be serious work, but everyone should enjoy it in some way.

The most important thing to do in selecting a project is to have the whole family spend time talking about it. Make sure each child and adult participates in the decision-making process. Here are some ideas for getting the discussion started:

1. Make a list of all the volunteering each member of the family is doing now. Would each parent or child want the other family members to help with any of these? (*Don't assume this to be self-evident. Allow each person the right to have individual interests and friends.*) Would other family members want to help with these?

2. What causes interest you, even if you are not sure what volunteer opportunities exist to help with them? Allow each family member to suggest a community problem of concern to him or her. If some of the ideas intrigue the whole family, start exploring what organizations are already working on these. Use the Internet, browse the Yellow Pages, go to the library, call the Volunteer Center. The search for the right community agency is part of the experience of volunteering as a family.

3. While it is important to identify causes and organizations to help, your family should also consider what tasks you most want to do. Make two lists. One for **Things We Know How To Do** and one for **Things We Would Like to Learn How to Do.** When you talk about the skills and talents you already have, be sure that something is listed for each family member. This is a great time for encouraging kids to acknowledge each others' and their parents' abilities. These lists will be very useful when you are ready to interview with an agency. See the worksheet on the next page.

It may take several sessions to complete the above steps. But the conversations should be revealing and positive.

Family Volunteering Worksheet

Our Family Members	Things we Know How to Do Already	Things We Would Like to Learn How to Do

Offering Your Services

Armed with your knowledge of your family's interests and talents, you are ready to offer yourselves as volunteers. While it makes sense to delegate one person to call for information and set up appointments, plan for all family members to interview together. Evaluate how comfortable the agency representative is in this type of group conversation because it is a clue as to whether or not the organization really wants the involvement of your children as well as the adults. Be sure everyone in your family speaks and has the chance to ask questions.

You may want to begin with a one-time activity. This will test the water to see how everyone likes volunteering together. There are many community events seeking people to help for a day—bazaars, clean-ups, painting parties, holiday activities. The agency with which you interview may have such an opportunity for your family as a pilot assignment.

Once you have committed to a volunteer project, take it seriously. Show your children that volunteer work is important and meaningful. Talk about the activity during the week and plan ahead to do it, even when things get hectic. Some of the volunteer work may introduce your children to new ideas and possibly to people different from themselves. What a wonderful opportunity for you to pass along your values and ethics—but only if you take time to talk about everyone's reactions. You, too, may discover many new things and be challenged by what you see. Share your personal feelings with your children.

When the time comes to complete the commitment or choose another project, involve the children in reaching closure. If things don't work out, show your children the right way to discuss your concerns with the organization. Because this should be a positive and *voluntary* experience for everyone, allow for some family members to change their interests over time.

As with so many other things in life, self-fulfilling prophecy works with volunteering, too. An enthusiastic attitude is infectious. Make sure everyone feels good about doing good!

Building for the Future

This guidebook has gone into great detail about ways to create volunteer opportunities for children. We have illustrated how children can volunteer as individuals, in groups, with family members, or with non-related adults. We have offered the viewpoint of youngsters themselves. We have described historical and current examples of youthful volunteering. Future examples will come from you!

Due to many complex factors, our society is experiencing a distancing of generations. What is referred to as the "generation gap" has some reality; adults and children often misunderstand and even fear each other. Therefore, a move towards involving youngsters in heretofore "adult" endeavors can only serve to break down stereotypes and barriers on both sides. By working together, adults and children learn to cooperate and respect each other's talents.

A fascinating prospect is the role volunteering can play in blending generations: children having the opportunity to be more "grown up" and adults having the opportunity to recapture the fresh perspective of childhood. Today, with so many working parents seeking ways to spend quality time with their children, volunteering as a family has a wide appeal. Adults can serve their community while spending time with their children, with the added benefit of modeling social responsibility.

Whether or not you structure your children's project according to the suggestions offered here is not as important as doing *something* to invite children into your corner of the volunteer world. The philosophic premise of *Children as Volunteers* is that youngsters under the age of fourteen are usually overlooked as a pool of talent. They are a volunteer recruitment resource available everywhere for those program leaders creative enough to recognize the potential.

As adults, we are the ones to teach children the importance of volunteering. We do support offering monetary payment for the usual types of simple "jobs" done by children (shoveling snow, walking dogs, etc.) because boys and girls should be prepared for the responsibilities of paid work. However, it is equally important to prepare children to perpetuate the tradition of volunteerism that has shaped American history. By participating in volunteer activities, youngsters learn the satisfaction and other benefits that come from freely offering their services to help others. Whatever it is called, when volunteering becomes a natural part of a child's life at an early age, it adds an important dimension to the process of growing up and, ultimately, shapes the adult that child becomes. Neither schoolwork nor salaried jobs teach *citizenship* in the hands-on way that volunteering does.

Our legal system assumes that children magically turn into "citizens" when they become old enough to vote, drink, drive, buy contraceptives, or serve in the military.

Yet what preparation have they really had for the responsibilities that citizenship entails? Volunteering is training for participatory democracy. And isn't it remarkable that youngsters can learn so much and be of real help at the same time?

In the 1980s, the administration of Pennsylvania Governor Casey recognized youngsters who participated in community service projects by asking them to take the following "Pledge of Citizenship":

> *I do solemnly swear that I will serve as an active citizen of my community, my state, and my country, and will accept equally the opportunities and duties of citizenship.*
>
> *I will support the Constitution and the laws of the United States of America and of the Commonwealth of Pennsylvania.*
>
> *I will participate actively as a self-governing member of our state and nation. When I am of voting age, I will register to vote and I will cast my ballot in every public election. I will inform myself about the problems of my community, my state, and my country, and will work with my fellow citizens to solve those problems.*
>
> *I will further act as a citizen through volunteer service to secure liberty and justice for all.*

Although most of the pledge takers were teenagers, the vision expressed applies to younger volunteers as well.

We urge you to look around and really *see* what children can accomplish when given the chance. Acknowledgment of children's help with fundraising events, neighborhood fairs, or school projects is a first step towards entrusting them with other types of community service. Take the second step! Act on the concept of the "self-fulfilling prophecy"—approach children as a source of innovation and energy, and you will rarely be disappointed. Believe in the idea. It does work, if you are open to the newness of it.

Appendix A
Interview/Survey Sources

The following are the locations at which we interviewed the approximately 350 youngsters referred to in this book. We are grateful to the children and their adult leaders for their willingness to offer input.

Boy Scout Troop, St. Michael's Association, Philadelphia, PA

Brownie Troop, St. Paul's Episcopal Church, Philadelphia, PA

Central High School, Philadelphia, PA

Clearview Elementary School, Stroudsburg, PA

Crossroads Community Center, Philadelphia, PA

East Lansdowne Basics School, East Lansdowne, PA

Ellwood Elementary School, Philadelphia, PA

First United Methodist Church of Germantown, Philadelphia, PA

George Washington Elementary School, Philadelphia, PA

Immaculate Conception School, Levittown, PA

Morrison Elementary School, Philadelphia, PA

Mother Bethel AME Church, Philadelphia, PA

Parkway Program, Philadelphia, PA

Saint Martin of Tours School, Philadelphia, PA

Samuel S. Fleischer Art Institute, Philadelphia, PA

Shaw Middle School, Philadelphia, PA

Stroudsburg Middle School, Stroudsburg, PA

Tenth Presbyterian Church, Philadelphia, PA

Valley Forge Intermediate School, Wayne, PA

YWCA, Mid-City Branch, Philadelphia, PA

Five children served as special "advisors" in the development of the book participating in the refining of the "think tank" concept: *Daniel Hecht, Jennifer Milles, Anne Monster, Elliot Weinbaum,* and *Laura Weinbaum.*

The individuals (or program representatives) named below spoke or wrote to us personally, generously sharing a great deal of information about their own experiences with children as volunteers. We thank them all.

Associates for Youth Development, Inc., Tucson, AZ

CATCH, Portland, OR

Center on Volunteerism, Adelphi University, Garden City, NY

Challenge Education Project, Indianapolis, IN

Children's Express, New York, NY

Children's Museum, Boston, MA

Cinekyd Enterprises, Hatboro, PA

Lynn Cohen, Shaw Middle School, Philadelphia, PA

Theresa Cunningham, Veterans Administration Medical Center, Grand Junction, CO

"The Customs Carried On" video project, College of Human Ecology, Cornell University, Ithaca, NY

Patricia Dodge, Silver Falls State Park, Sublimity, OR

Emeryville Junior Docent Program, Emeryville, CA

Beverly Evans, The Virginia Home, Richmond, VA

Jean Faber, Valley Forge Intermediate School, Wayne, PA

Dana Folsom, Bangor School District, Bangor, ME

Susan Foster, Coalition on Voluntarism, Wilmington, DE

Robert Gilbert, Lansdowne, PA

Barbara and Stuart Gilfillen, South Hamilton, MA

Ann A. Gilmore, Littleton, CO

Lee Gilmore, Denver, CO

Green Chimneys Farm Center, Brewster, NY

Lisa Griffin, Philadelphia, PA

Susan Grover, formerly of the Barrington Public Schools, Providence, RI

GUTS (Government Understanding for Today's Students), Intermediate School 139, Bronx, NY

Flo Hartman, Wayne, PA

Rev. Marsha L. B. Irmer, Lutheran Nursing Home, Brockton, MA

Linda T. Johnston, Citizen Involvement Division, City of Raleigh, NC

Stephanie Judson, Friends Select School, Philadelphia, PA

Junior Crime Fighters, Portland, OR

Junior Historian Club, Robert L. Vann School, Ahoskie, NC

Language to Share, Newton, MA

Magnolia Tree Earth Center of Bedford-Stuyvesant, Inc., Brooklyn, NY

Miriam R. Moore, New England Memorial Hospital, Stoneham, MA

Douglas L. Morgan, Youth Are Resources, Philadelphia, PA

Tracy Penn, Richmond, VA

Pennsylvania Institute for Youth Service, Philadelphia, PA

Project Math-Co, Wiscasset Middle School, Wiscasset, ME

Jeff Pryor, Partners, Inc., Denver, CO

Jill Schatkin, The Washington Home, Washington, DC

Mark Schechtman's Kids News, New York, NY

Carol Taylor, Voluntary Action Center of the Midlands, Columbia, SC

Arty Trost, Organizational Dynamics, Sandy, OR

West Rock Nature Center, New Haven, CT

Pam Wyrick, Greensboro Youth Council, Greensboro, NC

Appendix B
Resources & Bibliography

Information on Volunteer Management

There are a number of sources available for books, periodicals, and sample project materials on the subject of volunteer program development and management in general. To find these, start with your local Volunteer Center or visit the Energize, Inc. Web site at <http://www.energizeinc.com>. Energize will always provide you with the most updated volunteerism resource information and you can visit hundreds of links from there.

Information on Youth as Volunteers

Information on volunteer/community service projects for high school and college age young people is plentiful, but the body of knowledge on even younger volunteers is just beginning to grow. Don't neglect, however, organizations that deal with "older" youth. You may find ideas and suggestions that can be adapted to meet your needs in establishing volunteer programs for children under the age of fourteen.

The list below includes a sampling of national and regional sources providing publications and other information about youth as volunteers. In researching this revision of Children as Volunteers, we found their materials extremely relevant and are happy to share their names and addresses.

We particularly found the newsletters a treasure chest of information and have highlighted each of the titles. You will find valuable descriptions of existing youth volunteer programs, up-to-date information about relevant legislation and materials, as well as conference announcements.

Community Partnerships with Youth, Inc., 550 East Jefferson St., Suite 306, Franklin, IN 46131, (317) 736-7947, < http://www.cpyinc.org/>

A national training and resource development organization dedicated to promoting active citizenship through youth and adult partnerships.

Constitutional Rights Foundation, 601 S. Kingsley Drive, Los Angeles, CA 90005, (213) 487-5590. < http://www.crf-usa.org/>

A national leader in school youth service. Publishes videos, workbooks and other materials on programs, legislation and additional resources.

Innovation Center for Community and Youth Development, 7100 Connecticut Avenue, Chevy Chase, MD 20815, (301) 961-2837, < http://www.theinnovationcenter.org/>

An off-shoot of the National 4-H Council, The Innovation Center seeks, tests and promotes innovative concepts and practices in youth development.

National Youth Leadership Council, 1667 Snelling Avenue North, St. Paul, MN 55108 (651) 631-3672. < http://www.nylc.org/>

A major advocate for building vital, just communities with young people through service-learning and national service. Provides many print and Web resources.

Search Institute, The Banks Building, 615 First Avenue NE, Suite 125, Minneapolis, MN 55413, (612) 376-8955 or (800) 888-7828, <http://www.search-institute.org>

The Institute advances the well-being of adolescents and children and has developed the framework of 40 "developmental assets," which are positive experiences, relationships, opportunities, and personal qualities that young people need to grow up healthy, caring, and responsible. Publishes a variety of books and monographs.

Youth as Resources, 1000 Connecticut Ave., NW, 12th Floor, Washington, DC 20036, (202) 261-4131 < http://www.yar.org/>

As their Web site says: "Youth as Resources (YAR) is a philosophy and a program that recognizes youth as valuable community resources and engages them as partners with adults in bringing about positive community change."

Youth on Board, 58 Day Street Somerville, MA 02144, (617) 623-9900 x1242, <http://www.youthonboard.org/>

Youth on Board helps young people and adults think differently about each other so that they can work together to change society. Publishes books and has an informative Web site.

Youth Service America, 1101 15th Street, Suite 200, Washington, DC 20005, (202)296-2992, <http://www.ysa.org>

A resource center and alliance of 300+ organizations committed to increasing the quantity and quality of opportunities for young Americans to serve locally, nationally, or globally.

YouthWork Links and Ideas <http://www.youthwork.com/index.html>

Web site full of information for people working with children and teenagers, including dozen of links to other key sites.

Bibliography

Ellis, Susan J. *The Volunteer Recruitment (and Membership Development) Book, 3rd ed*. Philadelphia; Energize, 2002.

Ellis, Susan J. and Jayne Cravens, *The Virtual Volunteering Guidebook: How to Apply the Principles of Real-World Volunteer Management to Online Service*. <http://www.energizeinc.com/download/vvguide.pdf>

Ellis, Susan J. and Katherine Noyes Campbell. *By the People: A History of Americans as Volunteers, Third Edition*. Philadelphia: Energize, Inc., 2003.

Gilbert, Sara. *Lend a Hand: The How, Where and Why of Volunteering*. New York: Morrow Junior Books, 1988.

Lewis, Barbara A. *What Do You Stand For? A Kid's Guide to Building Character*. Minneapolis: Free Spirit Press, 1997.

McDuffie, Winifred G. and Judith R. Whiteman, eds. *Intergenerational Activities Program Handbook*. Intergenerational Activities Program, Broome County Child Development Council, Box 880, Binghamton, NY 13902. 1989.

Mosaic Youth Center Board of Directors with Jennifer Griffin-Wiesner. *Step-by-Step: A Young Person's Guide to Positive Community Change*. Minneapolis: Search Institute, 2001.

National Collaboration for Youth. *Screening Volunteers to Prevent Child Sexual Abuse: A Community Guide for Youth Organizations*. Washington, DC: The National Assembly of Health and Human Service Organizations, 1997.

National Commission on Resources for Youth. *An Introductory Manual on Youth Participation for Program Administrators*. Dept. of HEW Publication, #OHD/OYD 76-26045,1976.

Naylor, Harriet H. "Youth Volunteering." Speech given at the Southwest Regional Conference of the Child Welfare League of America, April 1977.

O'Neil, Jean. *Changing Perspectives: Youth as Resources*. Washington, DC: National Crime Prevention Council, 1990.

"Opportunities for Prevention: Building After School and Summer Programs for Young Adolescents." Children's Defense Fund Publication, Clearinghouse. July 1987.

Peyser, Hedy. "Involvement of 3- to 5-Year-Old Children as Volunteers." *Volunteer Administration*, Vol. XIII, No. 3, Fall 1980, pp. 39-44.

Popowski, Karen J. "Youth Views on Volunteering and Service Learning from the Chicago Area Youth Poll." *The Journal of Volunteer Administration*. Vol. III, No. 4, Summer, 1985, pp. 34-43.

Public/Private Ventures, *Youth Development: Issues, Challenges and Directions.* Philadelphia, Fall 2000. <http://www.ppv.org/content/reports/youthdevvolt.html>

Rolzinski, Catherine A. *The Adventure of Adolescence: Middle School Students and Community Se,vice.* Washington, DC, Youth Service America, 1990.

Sazama, Jenny and Karen S. Young. *Get the Word Out! Going Public about Young People's Power.* Somerville, MA: Youth on Board, 2001

Seidman, Anna and Jon Patterson. *Kidding Around? Be Serious! A Commitment to Safe Service Opportunities for Young People.* Washington, DC: Nonprofit Risk Management Center, 1996.

Skalka, Patricia. "The Kids Who Saved Fort Wayne." *Reader's Digest.* (December 1982), pp. 93-98.

Thoele, Mary. *Family Serve: Volunteer Opportunities for Families.* AAL Qualitylife Resources, 2001.

Walter, Virginia A. "Children as Citizens in Training: Political Socialization for a Strong Democracy," *Nonprofit and Voluntary Sector Quarterly*, Spring 1990, Vol. XIX, No. 1, pp. 7-18.

Weekly Reader, 200 First Stamford Place, P.O. Box 120023, Stamford, CT 06912, (203) 705-3500. <http://www.weeklyreader.com> (This classic elementary school publication promotes volunteering and other civic involvement.)